DELIVER US
FROM EVIL

HOW JESUS CASTS OUT
DEMONS TODAY

KENT PHILPOTT

EVP

Earthen Vessel Publishing

Deliver Us from Evil
How Jesus Casts Out Demons Today

Published 2014 by Earthen Vessel Publishing
San Rafael, CA 94903
www.evpbooks.com

Current edition ISBN: 978-0-9907277-0-5

First published 2009 by Earthen Vessel Publishing as
  How Christians Cast Out Demons Today
    (ISBN 978-0-9703296-3-9)
Library of Congress Control Number: 2014952983

Cover and Book Design by Katie L. C. Philpott

CONTENTS

Jesus said, pray then like this:

Our Father in heaven,
hallowed be you name.
Your kingdom come,
your will be done,
on earth as it is in heaven.
Give us this day our daily bread,
and forgive us our debts,
as we also have forgiven our debtors.
And lead us not into temptation,
but deliver us from evil.

PREFACE

At the time of my conversion to Christ in 1963, I was a junior in college. My major was psychology, and having embraced what I had been taught by my professors, I had trouble with certain segments of the Christian worldview, especially in regard to Satan and demons. I was not sure that the person of Satan as depicted in the Bible was something in which I even believed. The ideas of demons and demon possession were even more problematic, and I thought these were ancient and inaccurate descriptions of various forms of mental illness. That view dominated my thinking until I began living and ministering in San Francisco during the Jesus People Movement (1967-75). During that period, I was confronted with a stream of people who presented themselves in such a way that I had to conclude they had demons actually indwelling them. As a result, my views changed rather suddenly and became more closely aligned with that of the Gospel writers. It is a long story, and in what I hope to be a short and simple "how to" book about casting out of demons, I have decided to give accounts of only a few incidents that I think will help make essential points more concrete.

For ten years, from 1970 to 1980, in addition to leading a para-church ministry and pastoring a church, I operated the Marin Christian Counseling Center in San Rafael, California. Because I was unlicensed, I did not charge any fees but saw my work as a service to the community. In the process, I regularly conducted what came to be called a "deliverance ministry." In 1973, I wrote a book titled *A Manual of Demonology and the Occult*, originally to be a thesis for a ThM degree and published by Zondervan Publishing House (still available at Amazon.com). The publication of this book brought upon me an avalanche of ministry that I never anticipated and grew to dislike—many hundreds of people coming to my office and home, wanting deliverance from demons. It quickly became overwhelming and led to the publication of *The Deliverance Book*. The goal was to teach others, pastors and Christians in the pews, how to do the work of casting out of demons, so they would not show up at my door. Rather than egocentric, it was self-protective, an attempt to return to a normal life.

Though I will set forth a brief theology of the demonic, there will be no attempt to prove the existence of Satan and the demons. This generally takes care of itself. Admittedly, it is so other-worldly that I have sometimes wondered if all that contact with the demonic world really did take place. During that period it was routine to cast out demons, actually confronting demons directly, though not visibly apart from the persons they were indwelling.

In the years since the great outpouring of the Holy Spirit that sustained the Jesus People Movement, during what are called normal times as opposed to awakening times, there is some need to cast out demons, but to a far lesser extent. Nothing I experience now is anything close to what happened from 1967 to 1975. The difference between normal and awakening times appears to be quite significant. From 1967 to 1975, although I was not aware of this and did not appreciate nor understand what I was experiencing, there was, in my estimation, an outpouring of the Holy Spirit alongside which was a counterfeit and demonic outpouring of unclean spirit. Beyond stating this, I cannot explain it. That time was a period of awakening, but from that time to this, in the geographical region where I live and minister, it is normal time. Yes, some are converted, and there are occasions when demons are cast out, but to a much lesser degree than in times of awakening.

Recently, there seems to be an upsurge in the need to minister to those who recognize they have demons and want to trust in the person and work of Jesus Christ to be free of demonic influence and control. Frankly, I never wanted to return to this time-consuming and exhausting work. At a time when I have achieved some semblance of respectability in my community, it is less than an enticing prospect to express belief in the devil and all that is commonly associated with historic episodes like the Salem witchcraft trials. It is somewhat intimidating to live in a materialistic, rationally-oriented culture and be talking about casting out demons. Reality and the commission to serve our Lord Christ must, however, trump contemporary worldviews and personal apprehensions.

So it has come around once more in my life time—engaging in this risky business and once again finding it necessary to produce a little handbook on how to cast out demons. The worry of risk, however, is well-balanced by the motivation of the knowledge that Satan has deceived too many people and that Christians need to and can bring this ancient service to those who are willing to come to Jesus and His delivering touch.

A further declaration: I am an advocate of the Reformed tradition, which for me is most closely represented by the Canons of Dordt. (Google Canons of Dordt and you will find the position of the Dutch Reformed theologians over against the theology of Jacobus Arminius.) I am also pastor of Miller Avenue Baptist Church in Mill Valley, California, dually aligned with American and Southern Baptists. The question may arise as to whether I am a cessationist—someone who holds that the charismatic gifts of the Holy Spirit, especially the so-called power gifts like speaking in tongues and prophetic foretelling of the future, ceased with the publication of the New Testament. Or a similar question might be, am I a continuationist—one who believes the charismatic gifts continue into the present? " Semi-cessationist" or "semi-continuationist," probably both or either, describe my views. During normal times, when there is not a pronounced outpouring of the Holy Spirit in awakening or revival, I think the charismatic gifts are not as evident as when there is a time of awakening and revival. The casting out of demons, after all, does not involve any of the charismatic gifts as mentioned by Paul in Romans 12 or 1 Corinthians 12, with the possible exception of the gifts of faith and discernment.

The work at hand is not dictated by alignment with a particular theological camp. When I was theologically an Arminian, I engaged in the work of casting out of demons, and while now theologically Reformed, I engage in the work of casting out of demons.

Biblical quotes throughout this book are taken from The English Standard Version, published in 2001 by Crossway Bibles, a division of Good News Publishers. There is no perfect translation, and I have used many over the years, but the ESV is my current favorite.

"THE REASON THE SON OF GOD APPEARED WAS TO DESTROY THE WORKS OF THE DEVIL."
(1 JOHN 3:8B)

CHAPTER ONE

JESUS CASTS OUT DEMONS

With the advent of Jesus' ministry, the kingdom of God had come in person, and the unchecked and unrestrained reign of Satan had ended. The triumph of Jesus' passion, from crucifixion to resurrection and ascension, meant that Satan, though still present in the world, was destroyed in a way we do not completely understand. It is because of that victory over sin and Satan that Jesus extends to His Church authority even to cast out demons from people. The kingdom of God had come in the very person and presence of Jesus. The proof of this was demonstrated in His casting out of demons, by which it is traditionally thought that Jesus caused the demonic kingdom to tremble.

PRELIMINARY CONSIDERATIONS

In the Synoptic Gospels—Matthew, Mark, and Luke—there are six instances in which Jesus encountered demonized persons. There are other passages—Matthew 4:24, 8:16; Mark 1:32-34, 1:39, 3:11, 6:13; and Luke 4:41, 6:18, 7:2—which simply state that Jesus cast out demons as a part of his ministry. Mark 1:34 is representative of these passages: "And he healed many who were sick with various diseases, and cast out many demons. And he would not permit the demons to speak, because they knew him."

It has often been said that one third of Jesus' ministry involved the casting out of demons, the other two thirds being healing and preaching/teaching. Whether this is an accurate description of Jesus' ministry or not, we are reminded that Jesus did cast out demons, and He did commission His followers to do the same. (This commission will be examined in a later chapter.)

Note that healing and casting out of demons are not the same thing. Diseases will not be cast out. Physical illness or even mental illness requires healing, not the casting out of demons. While a person suffering from physical or mental illness may also be demonized, there is a fundamental difference between the two, although that difference is subtle. Even a wide and long involvement in deliverance ministry has not brought me full clarity about where one leaves off and the other begins. It still seems a mystery, and furthermore, it is not necessary to understand the nuances to engage in the work of casting out of demons.

Also note that the word "demonized" is the preferred term. It is not proper biblical terminology to describe someone as "demon-possessed." Jesus encountered people who had unclean spirits or demons, as we shall see, but possession is not the best word to describe these persons. To whatever degree or extent that the unclean spirit or demon operated in a person, total control is not what the Synoptic writers understood. Again, there is mystery here, yet it is not necessary to understand how a demon operates in a person in order to cast out that demon.

Jesus cast out or threw out demons. The word *ekballo* in the Greek of the New Testament means to "throw out" and is the word commonly used to describe Jesus' expelling of demons. We even get our term "ball," as in baseball, from this word. The prefix ek means "out," and "throw out" is what Jesus did. And, as we shall see, Jesus used no formulas, relics, rituals, ceremonies, or objects of any kind that might be associated with the practice of exorcism. Rather, in direct confrontation with unclean spirits indwelling the demonized, Jesus ordered or commanded demons to leave.

1. THE MAN WITH AN UNCLEAN SPIRIT AT A SYNAGOGUE IN CAPERNAUM

This event is found in Mark 1:21-27 and Luke 4:31-37:

> And they went into Capernaum, and immediately on the Sabbath he entered the synagogue and was teaching. And they were astonished at his teaching, for he taught them as one who had authority, and not as the scribes. And immediately there was in their synagogue a man with an unclean spirit. And he cried out, "What have you to do with us, Jesus of Nazareth? Have you come to destroy us? I know who you are— the Holy One of God." But Jesus rebuked him, saying, "Be silent, and come out of him!" And the unclean spirit, convulsing him and crying out with a loud voice, came out of him. And they were all amazed, so that they questioned among themselves, saying, "What is this? A new teaching with authority! He commands even the unclean spirits, and they obey him" (Mark 1:21-27).

ANALYSIS

The man had an unclean or unholy spirit, but it was a spirit, an entity separate and distinct from the mind, will, and person of the man. Jesus did not seek out the man with the unclean spirit; indeed, Jesus never sought out people with demons, but rather they came to or were brought to Him. It is unknown whether the man was a regular at the synagogue. How long Jesus was at the synagogue before the outburst occurred is unknown, although one might argue that Jesus had been teaching for some time and that the Sabbath service had concluded before the disruption started.

The unclean spirits began a conversation of sorts with Jesus. The unclean spirit(s) recognized Jesus as to His actual being and essence—the Holy One of God—and due to their uncleanness were threatened by His presence. That which is unholy reacted to and against that which was holy. The unclean spirits knew who Jesus was, although others did not; the demons knew He had the power to destroy them. It is as though they had anticipated Jesus the Christ's appearance. They recognized His authority even here, before His work was complete, before the resurrection and the glorification of the Lord of lords and King of kings. They cried out, giving the impression of chaos, but Jesus commanded them to be silent and directed them to come out of the demonized man. One demon acted as a representative of the group, but the grammar indicates there was more than one unclean spirit. The exit of the demons was not immediate; the unclean spirits convulsed the man—Luke says "threw him down"—then came out, crying out in loud voices.

Other attendees at the synagogue worship were amazed at what they had seen; this was entirely new to them. Authority over demons was startling to them, to say the least.

COMMENTS

Several points in the Gospel story are characteristic of my own experience. First, persons with unclean spirits will be present in gatherings dedicated to the teaching of Scripture and worship of God, but they are troubled at the presence of Jesus. Recall that we have the promise that where two or more are gathered because of Jesus, then He is also present (see Matthew 18:20).

Second, actual verbal confrontation with demons might take place; however, I suggest that Christians avoid such conversation. If Christians rely on what demons say, they may be misled or distracted. Some have gone so far as to suppose they are learning doctrinal truth from demons, but demons are liars and cannot ever be trusted or believed; therefore, conversation should be avoided. Jesus told them to be silent, and this is what I generally practice as well. Demons will not always quickly obey as they did in our story in Mark.

Third, demons are desperate and fight tenaciously to remain indwelt in a person. Nothing is out of bounds for an unclean spirit; they do not fight fairly. The convulsing is typical, along with other kinds of disturbances, and all are intended to short circuit the ministry. Demons can be scary to a degree, especially at first, and their intent is to unsettle those who would cast them out.

Seeing demons cast out or having demons cast out does not necessarily lead to faith in Christ. There is nothing in the story about the person becoming a disciple of Jesus. In fact, the event may have actually curtailed, or interfered, with the thrust of Jesus' ministry—that of teaching those He had called to Himself. Deliverance ministry is dramatic, and people are stirred up and excited, but this is not always a good thing. There was no exulting over or publishing of the account of the event in the synagogue by Jesus nor, we assume, by the apostles.

The demons talked to Jesus through the man, using that man's voice. Would the demons be talking to the man as well? In the last chapter I will speak of this in more detail, but it is likely that the demon carried on conversations with the individual. I have found this to be so time and again. And the issue is not one of hallucinations, which may accompany a disturbing event or be part of a psychotic episode. Having a hallucination and hearing voices are, in my view, not the same thing. An interesting point here, which is based on dozens of sessions of deliverance ministry and is my own observation: once the demon is cast out, there is no longer a conversation going on inside the formerly demonized person. The psychological and psychiatric communities are not likely to agreee with me on this, but I would submit the possibility for investigtion.

2. THE BLIND AND DUMB DEMONIAC

This event is found in Matthew 12:22-29, Mark 3:22-27, and Luke 11:14-22:

> Then a demon-oppressed man who was blind and mute was brought to him, and he healed him, so that the man spoke and saw. And all the people were amazed, and said, "Can this be the Son of David?" But when the Pharisees heard it, they said, "It is only by Beelzebul, the prince of demons that this man casts out demons." Knowing their thoughts, he said to them, "Every kingdom divided against itself is laid waste, and no city or house divided against itself will stand. And if Satan casts out Satan, he is divided against himself. How then will his kingdom stand? And if I cast out demons by Beelzebul, by whom do your sons cast them out? Therefore they will be your judges. But if it is by the Spirit of God that I cast out demons, then the kingdom of God has come upon you. Or, how can someone enter a strong man's house and plunder his goods, unless he first binds the strong man? Then indeed he may plunder his house (Matthew 12:22-29).

ANALYSIS

Matthew says that Jesus healed a demonized or demon-oppressed man who was blind and mute. Some translations have "demon-possessed," but the best rendering might be "demonized," which would mean that the physical disabilities were caused by demons in some unexplained manner. Apparently, Jesus cast out a demon, if we accept the evaluation of the Pharisees (see verse 24). Thus, we have a dual description: a man healed through the casting out of one or more demons. Healed can mean made whole regardless of the cause, which could either be disease as typically understood or the debilitating influence of a demonic spirit. Jesus' opponents did not question whether Jesus cast out a demon, but they resorted to the notion that it was the result of collusion with the prince of demons, Beelzebul. Jesus affirmed that He did in fact cast out demons. Verse 28 has a first class conditional clause (meaning that the statement is assumed to be true), with Jesus saying then that He did indeed cast out demons and by or through the Spirit of God (Luke 11:20 has "finger of God"). Thus, this activity was proof that the kingdom of God was present right there and then. The implication was that Jesus was the Messiah and King of the Kingdom. Jesus proved that He had power and authority over the strong man, Satan, and had just plundered his house by casting out a demon.

Mark has only a portion of the story, focusing on the accusation that Jesus casts out demons by the power of Beelzebul and does not mention an event of casting out demons. In Luke's account of the same story, there is no mention of healing but only that "he was casting out a demon that was mute" (Luke 11:14), and he does not mention the blindness. Verse 27 indicates that persons, probably not literally "sons" but students or persons associated with the Pharisees, engaged in expelling demons. In Acts 19:13-16 is the statement that "seven sons of a Jewish high priest named Sceva were doing this" (see v. 14). Knowing the covenant name of God, a name given by God to Moses in the burning bush incident of Exodus 3 (knowledge that might have been passed down to the high priest's family), was perhaps thought to give the one who used that name certain power over demons. In the Graeco-Roman world in general, which was rife with occultism, exorcism or occult versions of casting out demons were common. It was a for-profit business, and it was far different from what Jesus was doing. Here, however, Jesus forced his opponents to rethink the accusation against Him.

COMMENTS

On several occasions I witnessed that demonization resulted in physical disability, and that after a demon or demons were cast out, the disability vanished as well. I recall more than one instance when something that looked like a catatonic episode ended with demons being expelled. Apparently, a demon had so traumatized the person that he froze up and retreated as far from the real world as possible. Demons are extraordinarily fear-provoking to those who do not know how weak and foolish these unclean spirit beings actually are. It makes sense to me that blindness and muteness, without an organic cause, might be present in demonized persons.

One has to be careful here, however. It is unwise to think that many or most physical disorders have their root in the demonic. My research and experience suggests otherwise. The Christian minister must be careful not to suggest any more than what is plain and verifiable.

3. THE GADARENE DEMONIACS

This event is found in Matthew 8:28-34, Mark 5:1-20, and Luke 8:26-39:

And when he came to the other side, to the country of the Gadarenes, two demon-possessed men met him, coming out of the tombs, so fierce that no one could pass that way. And behold, they cried out, "What have you to do with us, O Son of God? Have you come here to torment us before the time?" Now a herd of many pigs was feeding at some distance from them. And the demons begged him, saying, "If you cast us out, send us away into the herd of pigs." And he said to them, "Go." So they came out and went into the pigs, and behold, the whole herd rushed down the steep bank into the sea and drowned in the waters. The herdsmen fled, and going into the city they told everything, especially what had happened to the demon-possessed man. And behold, all the city came out to meet Jesus, and when they saw him, they begged him to leave their region (Matthew 8:28-34).

ANALYSIS

Two technical points must be made: one, the location (or the name of the location) of the event differs amongst the Gospel writers. Matthew has the country of the Gadarenes, Mark and Luke the country of the Gerasenes. This is an interesting problem, not unsolvable, but not germane to this treatise. Two, Matthew has two demonized men, but Mark and Luke have just one. The reconciliation may be that there were two, as Matthew recounts, but only one who spoke, or that only one became a disciple of Jesus. Mark and Luke state that a single man approached Jesus and at least bowed before Him, although he did not actually worship Him. In both Mark and Luke, the man, now in his right mind and free of the demons, wanted to become a follower or disciple of Jesus and to travel with Him. In any case, the number of the men may have been irrelevant to the purposes of Mark and Luke in their telling of the story.

As in the previous event, the men are described as demonized or demon-oppressed or -influenced. They were fierce and extraordinarily strong, according to Mark 5:4, and they lived in the tombs apart from other people.

The demons inhabiting the men conversed with Jesus. Mark relates that Jesus actually requested the name of the demon, who told him the name was Legion, perhaps meaning there were many demons in the man (Mark 5:9). The demons, as in the story of the man with an unclean spirit at the synagogue (Mark 1:21-28), also recognized who Jesus was and knew they had reason to fear Him, because Jesus could actually cast them out of the men. The demons even begged Jesus to send them into the pigs. The "if" in Matthew 8: 31 is in the first class condition, meaning that the demons knew Jesus could and would cast them out. No explanation is given by any of the Gospel writers for this request, nor is any given for Jesus' granting the request.

COMMENTS

Conversing with demons is something I was prone to do early on in my encounters with the demonized. I thought I was learning a great many things. And I did ask demons for their names, particularly when the work was tedious and exhausting. The idea has been from ancient times that to know the name of a demon means having power over the demon. Such was not always the case, and I rarely attempt this now. Conversation with demons should be avoided, and it is sometimes difficult to know exactly with whom one is conversing. Demons will try almost anything. I have had demons attempt to flatter me, accuse me, dismiss me, disregard me, and even tell me things about myself that no one else knew. It is best to avoid conversing with or believing unclean spirits, because demons are liars and deceivers.

Demons do not want to be cast out of flesh. I do not understand this, but it might be that to be cast out of flesh would result in being sent into hell itself. Hell may be a spiritual realm and not in time or space at all. As an adversary of God and His creation, Satan would be barred in hell from all contact with God's creation.

Demonized persons can be incredibly strong and fierce, which I have witnessed many times. However, despite being attacked by demonized people, I have never once been injured or even marked, even after being hit full in the face by large, powerful, demonized men. I cannot explain this, but vivid memories still linger. Early on in my ministry I would, in a sense, allow the struggles. But then I came to see it as error and no longer engage in wrestling matches—I mean, literal wrestling matches. "Be silent!" or "Stop!" is usually enough.

Jesus, the Holy One of God, brings fear to demons and also to any one of us sinful people, and so the local people begged Jesus to depart from them. Demons tremble at the person (name) of Jesus, but they rarely tremble at His disciples. This is why Jesus is the one who casts out the demons.

4. THE DAUGHTER OF A CANAANITE WOMAN

This event is found in Matthew 15:21-28 and Mark 7:24-30:

> And Jesus went away from there and withdrew to the district of Tyre and Sidon. And behold, a Canaanite woman from that region came out and was crying, "Have mercy on me, O Lord, Son of David; my daughter is severely oppressed by a demon." But he did not answer her a word. And his disciples came and begged him, saying "Send her away, for she is crying out after

us." He answered, "I was sent only to the lost sheep of the house of Israel." But she came and knelt before him, saying, "Lord, help me." And he answered, "It is not right to take the children's bread and throw it to the dogs." She said, "Yes, Lord, yet even the dogs eat the crumbs that fall from their master's table." Then Jesus answered her, "O woman, great is your faith! Be it done for you as you desire." And her daughter was healed instantly (Matthew 15:21-28).

ANALYSIS

The story is not one of casting out of demons; that part of it is entirely secondary. At issue is Jesus' ministry to a non-Jew—a Canaanite and a woman, a resident of the district of Tyre and Sidon (Syrophoenicia). The mother of the victim told Jesus that her daughter was severely oppressed by a demon. It is not clear that an actual demon was involved, since we have only the mother's opinion, and people of that time and culture attributed much to demons. Jesus does not directly corroborate the woman's analysis of the situation, and there is no language that suggests there was a casting out of a demon; rather the daughter was healed. The healing was accomplished from a distance and happened suddenly. The Greek word here is *iathe*, an aorist passive from *iaomai* and can mean heal, cure, and restore.

COMMENTS

It does the Scripture no dishonor to suggest that the story of the Canaanite woman is not about the casting out of a demon. Only the woman's statement indicates any demon involvement at all. Jesus does not contradict her, making it possible that Jesus assented to the diagnosis. But we cannot be sure.

My interest here is to bring out the essential difference

between physical healing and casting out of demons. As far as I understand Scripture, and as far as I understand my own experiences, physical disease is healed, but demons are cast out. I tend to be skeptical about reported miracles, but I have witnessed healings, have been healed myself, and have, through my own activity according to biblical passages such as James 5:14-15, seen people healed right in front of me. My college major was psychology, and I am aware of the nature of psychosomatic illness and other related phenomena. Healing of actual, organically-based illness is something other than casting out of demons. The two should not be confused.

There are other conditions that are not "cast out." I have read reports of casting out demons of addiction and homosexuality—whether there are such I am not sure—but addictions and same sex attraction are not ended through a deliverance ministry or any other quick fix.

5. THE EPILEPTIC BOY

This event is found in Matthew 17:14-21, Mark 9:14-29, and Luke 9:37-43:

> And when they came to the crowd, a man came up to him and kneeling before him said, "Lord, have mercy on my son, for he is an epileptic and he suffers terribly. For often he falls into the fire and often into the water. And I brought him to your disciples, and they could not heal him. And Jesus answered, "O faithless and twisted generation, how long am I to be with you? How long am I to bear with you? Bring him here to me." And Jesus rebuked him, and the demon came out of him, and the boy was healed instantly. Then the disciples came to Jesus privately and said, "Why could we not cast it out?" He said to them, "Because of your

little faith. For truly, I say to you, if you have faith like a grain of mustard seed, you will say to this mountain, 'Move from here to there,' and it will move, and nothing will be impossible for you" (Matthew 17:14-21).

ANALYSIS

A threshold question is, was the boy in the story an epileptic? Or, was the boy's father mistaken, and the physical effects of a demonic presence only looked like epilepsy in the understanding of the people of that era? It should be noted that Jesus did not confirm the father's diagnosis. Also, Mark recorded the father as saying that his son had a "dumb spirit" and Luke a "spirit." In Luke's Gospel the father asks the disciples to cast out a demon, while in Matthew the father asks for a healing. Mark states that the "spirit saw him" (Mark 9:20). Most significant, however, is that Matthew affirms that the "demon came out of him."

The indication, therefore, is that a demon was at the core of the boy's trouble. Jesus rebuked a demon, it came out of the boy, and the boy was healed or made whole. The casting out of a demon resulted in a healing—the connection between a demon being cast out and healing being significant. It might be concluded that epilepsy was a misdiagnosis.

The disciples could not cast out the demon, due, Jesus said, to a lack of faith (in Matthew) and to a lack of prayer (in Mark). The best manuscripts do not have verse 21, "But this kind never comes out except by prayer and fasting." It is possible that fasting may reflect a period in the Church when casting out of demons had become ritualized through a process of exorcism. Faith and prayer in the verses under consideration do not have stated objects—faith in what or whom, prayer about what and to whom.

In Mark and Luke, the demon attacked the boy before it

came out, and according to Mark, after casting out the demon, Jesus ordered the demon to never enter the boy again (Mark 9:25). The demon was successfully cast out once the boy was brought to Jesus.

COMMENTS

The connection between physical illness and demonization is a puzzle. While physical or emotional illness cannot be cast out, demonic activity in a person may appear to be organic or mental in origin. On the other hand, symptoms of the illness may be a side effect of the demonic activity. The way a demon works in a person is mysterious, and it is probable that only God knows the exact processes, and it is enough that God knows.

Prayer is to be directed to our God, trusting in or having faith in the person and finished work of Jesus Christ, who has destroyed the work of the devil. Little will be accomplished when disciples of Jesus suppose they are acting on their own power and authority. People with demons must be brought to Jesus. When two or more of us gather together on account of Him, Jesus is there with us, and He is able to do the work.

That Jesus ordered the demon never to enter the boy again has been a mystery to me, and I wonder whether I should do the same and whether I am warranted to voice something only Jesus was reported to say. But right or wrong, I do make such statements. In the work of casting out demons, we sometimes are unsure of what to do and what to say; I have thought that the less done and said the better.

6. A WOMAN WITH A DISABLING SPIRIT

This event is found in Luke 13:10-17:

> Now he was teaching in one of the synagogues on the Sabbath. And there was a woman who had had a

disabling spirit for eighteen years. She was bent over and could not fully straighten herself. When Jesus saw her, he called her over and said to her, "Woman, you are freed from your disability." And he laid his hands on her, and immediately she was made straight, and she glorified God. But the ruler of the synagogue, indignant because Jesus had healed on the Sabbath, said to the people, "There are six days in which work ought to be done. Come on those days and be healed, and not on the Sabbath day." Then the Lord answered him, "You hypocrites! Does not each of you on the Sabbath untie his ox or his donkey from the manger and lead it away to water it? And ought not this woman, a daughter of Abraham whom Satan bound for eighteen years, be loosed from this bond on the Sabbath day?" As he said these things, all his adversaries were put to shame, and all the people rejoiced at all the glorious things that were done by him (Luke 13:10-17).

ANALYSIS

It is Luke who says "disabling spirit," while Jesus says only "disability." The threshold question again is whether a demon is involved, or whether the woman's condition is a physical illness, perhaps osteoporosis. Jesus does state that Satan had bound the woman (v. 16), but no demon is explicitly cast out.

Jesus laid hands on the woman, a practice associated with physical healing. This is a story of a healing, but the healing is only incidental to the story's primary message regarding Sabbath regulations, an issue that Jesus confronts often and may have been the reason Jesus initiated the contact with the woman in the first place.

If there was a disabling spirit involved, then this is a casting out of demons. But if the quasi-medical term, disabling spirit, is only a generalized description of a kind that Dr. Luke might employ, then there is no casting out of demons. Which it is, I propose is unknowable.

COMMENTS

It does not seem that there are any clear-cut principles about casting out of demons here, though on rare occasions I witnessed that physical symptoms did seem to disappear after demons were cast out.

Unique to this story is that Jesus approached the woman who was in distress rather than the other way around. Whether or not the story involves the demonic, it is not advisable that Christian workers approach the demonized in as direct a fashion as Jesus did. The principle seems to be that the demonized come to Jesus or to His disciples first. I have found myself in considerable trouble by initiating such ministry. Perhaps I am overly cautious here, but in a day of lawsuits and other complaints, propriety is often best.

CHAPTER TWO

JESUS' DISCIPLES CAST OUT DEMONS

It is plain that Jesus cast out demons, but did anyone else do so? If Jesus was the only one who cast out demons, then how can we be certain this is a legitimate ministry for today?

Down through the centuries, accounts of exorcism, as it came to be called, made their way into numerous church histories. In the Jesus People Movement of the 1960s and 1970s, the casting out of demons was commonplace, and I was very much involved in that work. However, our concern here is what we find in our sole authority, the Bible, which is the only sure foundation for such a critical service as deliverance from unclean spirits. This chapter will therefore be limited to the early church's history as we find it in the New Testament.

THE SENDING OUT OF THE APOSTLES AND THE SEVENTY-TWO

> And he called the twelve together and gave them power and authority over all demons and to cure diseases, and he sent them out to proclaim the king-

dom of God and to heal (Luke 9:1-2). After this the Lord appointed seventy-two others and sent them on ahead of him, two by two, into every town and place where he himself was about to go (Luke 10:1). The seventy-two returned with joy, saying, "Lord, even the demons are subject to us in your name!" And he said to them, "I saw Satan fall like lightning from heaven. Behold, I have given you authority to tread on serpents and scorpions, and over all the power of the enemy, and nothing shall hurt you. Nevertheless, do not rejoice in this, that the spirits are subject to you, but rejoice that your names are written in heaven" (Luke 10:17-20).

ANALYSIS

Jesus sent out the twelve Apostles on what was first and foremost a preaching mission. At the same time, He gave them both power and authority over all demons and power and authority to cure diseases. "Heal" at the end of verse 9:2 is the usual word for physical healing and not the word we get our English "therapy" from, which has the sense of making whole and may be used to describe both the casting out of demons and physical healing. Healing illness and casting out of demons were signs that the kingdom of God had come.

The point is that Jesus gave the apostles power and authority over demons, so we assume they did cast out demons. But then seventy-two others, not including the twelve apostles, were sent out as well. No statement is made as to their having been given power and authority to cast out demons or to heal, but when the thirty-six pairs returned, they reported with joy that even the demons were subject to them; that is, they were able to cast them out. So we see that disciples of Jesus other than the apostles cast out demons.

COMMENTS

It is clearly established that persons other than Jesus cast out demons. The apostles cast out demons, and a certain un-named disciple of Jesus did so as well (see below). What is not clarified is whether the power and authority over demons is extended to those beyond these eighty-four persons. Systems of thought have emerged in the history of the Church stating divergent opinions, often in direct contradiction to one another, but to dogmatically argue for one way or another is to go beyond the plain statements of Scripture.

The Twelve were given power and authority over all demons. The power and authority belonged to Jesus, but He gave it to them. The question is then, do we today have power and authority over demons in the same way the Twelve did? Scripture convinces me that the answer is yes. The power and authority was not their own, but was given to them by Jesus in an act of commissioning. Since Pentecost, a born again Christian is indwelt by Jesus' Holy Spirit. Jesus did not leave us alone but sent the Helper to be with us forever (see John 14). The indwelling Holy Spirit means that Jesus is with us, and according to 1 John 4:4, "He who is in you is greater than he who is in the world." This is certainly a mystery, but Jesus is with us, and He is the One with power and authority over all demons. This is basis enough to give warrant for Christians casting out demons today.

Jesus' warning to avoid being engulfed by an unhealthy sense of being empowered—that they had power and authority over demons—was something I had to deal with personally. It was somewhat intoxicating to suddenly discover that demons would obey me. If anything, this is an understatement, for this tendency is a serious issue. It must be borne in mind that casting out demons is a service extended to demon-tormented persons who are yet loved of God, performed by those who have barely escaped the torment of hell themselves.

THE UNKNOWN MAN WHO CAST OUT DEMONS

In both Mark 9:38-41 and Luke 9:49-50 is the story of some-one who was casting out demons in the name of Jesus:

> John said to him, "Teacher, we saw someone casting out demons in your name, and we tried to stop him, because he was not following us." But Jesus said, "Do not stop him, for no one who does a mighty work in my name will be able soon afterward to speak evil of me. For the one who is not against us is for us. For truly, I say to you, whoever gives a cup of water to drink because you belong to Christ will by no means lose his reward" (Mark 9:38-41).

ANALYSIS

Both the apostle John and Jesus affirm that the unknown man was casting out demons. Jesus called it a "mighty work." There is no suggestion that the man was merely trying to perform an exorcism with magician's tricks or illusions. Perhaps the man had witnessed Jesus casting out demons and thought he should then use the name of Jesus in his own work, which would not have been much different from the activities of the seven sons of Sceva of Acts 19. Perhaps the unknown man had witnessed Jesus' apostles casting out demons, since Luke does place this story after the sending out of the twelve as recorded in Luke 9.

Jesus would not allow His own followers to stop the man from doing his ministry and indicates that the man was not working against but for them. He went further and implied that the man would receive a reward.

COMMENTS

The unknown man, who has remained unknown through-out history, was not an apostle; he was not one of the seventy-two of Luke 10. He did not directly receive a commission from Jesus to cast out demons. It is likely that he simply imitated what he saw Jesus do. This is very close to what Jesus' followers have done throughout the ages—cast out demons because of what they read in the New Testament.

"In your name" was the phrase used by the disciples to describe what the unknown disciple was doing. This phrase means that the man was trusting or depending on the person of Jesus for authority over the demons. The phrase was not used as a magical formula. Merely uttering the words "in the name of Jesus" is nothing at all. In that day, exorcists would use various formulas full of what were thought to be powerful, magical names to control evil spirits.

SIGNS AND WONDERS IN THE EARLY CHURCH

Luke summarizes activities of the primitive Church, the Church very close in time to the events of the Day of Pentecost, in Acts 5:12-17. Of special significance for our subject is verse 16:

> The people also gathered from the towns around Jerusalem, bringing the sick and those afflicted with unclean spirits, and they were all healed (Acts 5:16).

ANALYSIS

Diseased persons and those with unclean spirits were brought to the apostles (see verse 12) for very good reasons—they needed healing. Healed here carries the idea of being made whole, and can apply to both physical healing

and/or casting out demons. The apostles evidently contin-
ued the ministry they had learned from Jesus.

COMMENTS
The apostles experienced the continuation of signs and wonders that characterized the ministry of Jesus, and these signs
and wonders pointed to something beyond themselves, to
the person and office of Jesus Christ. This is the proper view
of casting out of demons. Jesus is honored and lifted up as
people are delivered from demonic influence.

THE MINISTRY OF PHILIP IN SAMARIA

Now those who were scattered went about preaching
the word. Philip went down to the city of Samaria and
proclaimed to them the Christ. And the crowds with
one accord paid attention to what was being said by
Philip when they heard him and saw the signs that he
did. For unclean spirits came out of many who were
possessed, crying with a loud voice, and many who
were paralyzed or lame were healed. So there was
much joy in that city (Acts 8:4-8).

ANALYSIS
This is not the apostle Philip, but the Philip of Acts 6:5, one of
the seven chosen in order to set the Twelve free from serving
tables. Whether he was one of the seventy-two of Luke 10 is
unknown. Because of the first real persecution of the Church
that erupted following the stoning of Stephen, many believers in Jesus, except the apostles, left Jerusalem. One of these
was Philip, who traveled to Samaria. He preached Christ in
the city of Samaria, and the signs that accompanied Philip's
ministry helped open hearts and minds. The signs are that
those having unclean spirits had them come out of them,

and diseased persons were healed or made whole. The ESV, along with most other versions, has "possessed" in verse 7, but a better reading would be "having unclean spirits." The result was much joy.

COMMENTS
Philip was not an apostle but a servant in the early Church on whom the apostles had laid their hands (see Acts 6:6). This laying on of hands must not be viewed as giving Philip magical powers but as commissioning and affirming him.

Unclean spirits came out crying with loud voices. My experience matches this description. The person with the unclean spirit cries out, but it is actually a demon provoking this. I assume that the demon uses the vocal cords of the person indwelt by the demon. The crying out and the loud voices are things that have long puzzled me. Perhaps it is to frighten the minister or the person with the unclean spirit, in order to short circuit or curtail the deliverance ministry. Perhaps it is an expression of the utter horror of the demon who is being destroyed by the Holy One of God (see Mark 1:24).

THE SLAVE GIRL WITH A SPIRIT OF DIVINATION

As we were going to the place of prayer, we were met by a slave girl who had a spirit of divination and brought her owners much gain by fortune-telling. She followed Paul and us, crying out, "These men are servants of the Most High God, who proclaim to you the way of salvation." And this she kept doing for many days. Paul, having become greatly annoyed, turned and said to the spirit, "I command you in the name of Jesus Christ to come out of her." And it came out that very hour. But when her owners saw that their hope of gain was gone, they seized Paul and Silas and dragged them into the marketplace before the rulers (Acts 16:16-19).

ANALYSIS

In the course of their work in the Greek city of Philippi, Paul and Silas met a slave girl, who had an unclean spirit—although Luke leaves out the adjective "unclean"—that enabled the girl to tell fortunes. She and/or the spirit knew who Paul and Silas were—servants of the Most High God—which is reminiscent of other unclean spirits who knew who Jesus was when humans did not. Paul became annoyed and confronted the spirit rather than the girl, commanding the spirit to come out "in the name of" (or because of or due to the power and authority of) Jesus Christ. Luke states that "it came out that very hour." The language may be taken to mean that either the spirit came out at once or that it took only a short time. The evidence that the spirit came out is that the girl was no longer able to tell fortunes. This event occurred in the open with people watching; the results were visible and dramatic and caused further consequences.

COMMENTS

Paul with Silas cast out a demon. Nowhere is there a direct statement that Jesus had given Paul power and authority to cast out unclean spirits, but Paul did cast them out. We might expect that this occurred more than once. Unclean spirits recognize and react to the presence of Jesus Christ, the Holy One of God, which I have witnessed many times. On several occasions, demons have recognized me and have said things about me, some of which I would not have wanted known. During my ministry, these unclean spirits have not always departed immediately, which is one reason why the work can be tiring. But like Paul's, the basic approach is to command spirits to come out, while depending solely on the person and work of Jesus Christ to effect the results.

One of the difficulties involved in casting out demons is that those who are indwelt by them may not want them to leave. Demons provide a broad variety of apparent benefits for people, like the ability to tell fortunes. A demon will intimidate a person by repeatedly warning of the loss should it be expelled. This is a clever and highly effective tactic. A person must (usually) want to be free of the unclean spirits before deliverance is possible.

THE SEVEN SONS OF SCEVA

> And God was doing extraordinary miracles by the hands of Paul, so that even handkerchiefs or aprons that had touched his skin were carried away to the sick, and their diseases left them and the evil spirits came out of them. Then some of the itinerant Jewish exorcists undertook to invoke the name of the Lord Jesus over those who had evil spirits, saying, I adjure you by the Jesus whom Paul proclaims." Seven sons of a Jewish high priest named Sceva were doing this. But the evil spirit answered them, "Jesus I know, and Paul I recognize, but who are you?" And the man in whom was the evil spirit leaped on them, mastered all of them and overpowered them, so that they fled out of that house naked and wounded (Acts 19:11-16).

ANALYSIS

Miraculous, extraordinary healings of a type that astonish and leave us with major questions, and "evil" spirits being cast out—these are events that go beyond the more ordinary Gospel accounts of Jesus' casting out of demons. "Evil" in this passage is from a word that can mean sick, but here, as is commonly done, it is translated in an ethical sense of bad or evil, another way of saying unclean.

Like the unknown man of Mark 9 and Luke 9, we find people who apparently presented themselves as exorcists, who were attempting to cast out demons by pronouncing the name of Jesus Christ, perhaps in imitation of the ministry of Paul. These seven sons of Sceva were probably professional exorcists capitalizing on a popular notion that, since they were connected with a high priest of Israel, they would know the secret covenant name of God and this would therefore give them special spiritual powers. Their formula of "I adjure you" was not and is not a Christian or biblical statement but would be characteristic of occult-oriented exorcists.

The evil spirit knew who Jesus was, but it was merely acquainted with Paul. Luke makes the distinction clear. While the demon did know Jesus, whose name they were attempting to use magically, it yielded no power to the exorcists, and it overwhelmed them in a most dramatic and shameful manner, utterly exposing them.

COMMENTS

Over the course of my ministry, I have seen events that parallel to some lesser degree that which Luke relates. Demons who are powerful and will not be controlled, demons who know who Jesus is but will mock those who are pretenders, and occultists who seem to be spiritually powerful but ultimately are not— these situations I have seen numerous times.

Some of what is related of Paul's ministry in Ephesus is beyond my comprehension, but in a city like ancient Ephesus, so inundated with occult practices, wild and strange scenes would likely have taken place. There is a bewildering element to the work of casting out demons; it really is not for the faint of heart or nerve.

THE ABILITY TO DISTINGUISH BETWEEN SPIRITS

Among the varieties of gifts given by God is the ability to distinguish between spirits (1 Corinthians 12:19). This gift is mentioned nowhere else in the New Testament. It is sometimes assumed that the distinguishing or discerning has to do with knowing whether demons are involved or not, or it may be that the gift has to do with understanding the difference between orthodox and heterodox doctrines. Then again, it may be that both are true. I have not come to a position on this issue.

Perhaps Philip had this gift in Samaria; maybe Paul had it in Philippi and Ephesus. Perhaps this gift may help explain the ministry of Jesus to those who had unclean spirits. When Jesus commissioned the Twelve and later the seventy-two, there is no mention of a spiritual gift being given. My point is that some link the casting out of demons with the charismatic gifts and therefore dismiss the ministry out of hand. But I see no scriptural warrant for that position. In my own case, being correct in an assessment about whether a person had a demonic spirit or whether demons were involved at all was not a sure thing.

If the concept of cessationism—that the charismatic gifts of the Holy Spirit have ceased to be operative in the Church, especially speaking in tongues and prophetic foretelling—were accurate, this would still not negate the fact that Christians can cast out demons today.

CONCLUDING REMARKS

Though there are passages in the epistles that speak of Satan and the demonic, there are no other clear-cut passages that deal specifically with the casting out of demons. Paul writes of our warfare as not being against flesh and blood but against the demonic kingdom (Ephesians 6:12), and Peter speaks of Satan being like a roaring lion seeking someone to devour (1 Peter 5:8). There are other mentions of the demonic, especially in Revelation.

My view is that there is nothing in Scripture that would prohibit Christians from engaging in the casting out of demons. Neither is there anything in Scripture that explicitly instructs it. Again, in the letters of the New Testament, no acts of casting out demons are described. Perhaps it was considered normative and did not need discussing, or perhaps the need had largely disappeared, like it usually does during normal times. However, it is clear that casting out demons was not limited to the twelve Apostles, and there is nothing limiting casting out demons to first century Christians or to those Christians living during the formation of the New Testament.

One eschatological (end times or last things) theory has Satan being bound during a thousand year reign of Christ, which is seen as a metaphor for the established victory of Christ and extends from the Resurrection to the Second Advent of Christ. In my view, this theory would not preclude demonization but would mean that Christians could cast out unclean spirits, because these demons have been defeated though the work of Jesus. Whatever one's view of last things might be, casting out demons by disciples of Jesus should be understood as normative.

We are now ready to move toward a brief history of casting out demons after the era of the New Testament, then a brief discussion of the theology of the demonic. Then after two other brief chapters, we will look at how Christians may go about a ministry of casting out demons today.

CHAPTER THREE

CASTING OUT DEMONS AFTER THE NEW TESTAMENT ERA

Most of our information about casting out demons in the first century comes from Matthew, Mark, and Luke, including the book of Acts. John's Gospel has no direct mention of casting out demons, and the same can be said of the letters of Paul, Peter, James, Jude, and John. Neither is there anything pertaining to the subject in Hebrews or Revelation. It is as though casting out demons and healing—the two signs and wonders common to Jesus' ministry—had disappeared after about AD 70. This conclusion is based largely on silence or lack of information and not on actual events.

The earliest mention of casting out of demons may be found in the longer ending of the Gospel of Mark:

> And these signs will accompany those who believe: In my name they will cast out demons; they will speak in new tongues; they will pick up serpents with their hands; and if they drink any deadly poison, it will not hurt them; they will lay their hands on the sick, and they will recover (Mark 16:17-18).

This longer ending of Mark with its mention of casting out demons does not appear in the major manuscripts of the New Testament until the fourth century, maybe the fifth century. However, it is generally considered that the long ending may have originated late in the second century. Though not considered original to Mark's Gospel, it still gives evidence that Christians were casting out demons after the publication of the New Testament. It is also noted that the term "exorcism" is not used in the long ending of Mark; rather, a variation of the normative New Testament phrase, "throwing out of demons," is found. The ending reflects an early understanding of casting out of demons as opposed to later accounts where "exorcism" is the word chiefly used.

JUSTIN MARTYR

In the second century, Justin Martyr (ca. 100-165) wrote that Christians in his day commonly exorcized·demons, and they did it in the name of Jesus.

Justin was an apologist for the Christian Faith, in that he defended Christianity by setting forth the essential message of the Church. The focus of his defense was the incarnation—God had become flesh in the person of Jesus Christ. He also wrote of demons. In the First Apology, chapter XXVIII, Justin spoke of God's care for men:

> For among us the prince of the wicked spirits is called the serpent, and Satan, and the devil, as you can learn by looking into our writings. And that he would be sent into the fire with his host, and the men who follow him, and would be punished for an endless duration, Christ foretold. For the reason why God has delayed to do this, is His regard for the human race.

Justin wrote at a time when it was necessary to outline

the essential biblical doctrines, since there were few who had any access to the primary Christian Scriptures. It is plain that Justin had a normative biblical view of Satan. Justin also spoke of demons:

> For He was made man also, as we before said, having been conceived according to the will of God the Father, for the sake of believing men, and for the destruction of the demons. And now you can learn this from what is under you own observation. For numberless demoniacs throughout the whole world, and in your city, many of our Christian men exorcising them in the name of Jesus Christ, who was crucified under Pontius Pilate, have healed and do heal, rendering helpless and driving the possessing devils out of the men, though they could not be cured by all the other exorcists, and those who used incantations and drugs (Second Apology, chapter VI).

It is noted that Justin did not use the term "casting out of demons" but rather the standard term of the day, "exorcism." Alhough the term "exorcism" is employed by Justin, it would be synonymous with the more biblical term, "casting out of demons." It would be a century before the practice of casting demons out became corrupted into something more closely resembling pagan and occult practices. Justin distinguished here between Christian exorcism and the magic-oriented exorcism common to his time. In his Dialogue with Trypho, chapter 85:3, this is affirmed:

> For every demon, when exorcized in the name of this very Son of god—who is the First-born of every creature, who became man by the Virgin, who suffered, and was crucified under Pontius Pilate by your nation,

who died, and ascended into heaven—is overcome and subdued. But though you exorcize any demon in the name of any of those who were amongst you—either kings, or righteous men, or prophets, or patriarchs—it will not be subject to you.

Justin reminds Trypho, a Jewish philosopher, that although there were Jewish exorcists about, they were not able to do what the Christian exorcists could do. The point here is that in the middle to the third quarter of the second century, Christians were successfully casting demons out of people.

IRENAEUS OF LYONS

A bishop in Lyons, France, during the probable dates of AD 120-202 and therefore writing roughly a half-century later than Justin, Irenaeus demonstrated a continuing biblical view of the casting out of demons. His principle writing was *A Refutation and Subversion of Knowledge Falsely So Called*, but more popularly known as *Against Heresies*. *Against Heresies* is composed of five books, and quotes are cited with formulas such as (Haer. 2.31.2) which follows:

For they can neither confer sight on the blind, nor hearing on the deaf, nor chase away all sorts of demons—(none, indeed,) except those that are sent into others by themselves, if they can even do so much as this. Nor can they cure the weak, or the lame, or the paralytic, or those who are distressed in any other part of the body as has often been done in regard to bodily infirmity.

Irenaeus, writing against two contemporary prominent Gnostics, Simon and Carpocrates, contrasts the ministry of the Gnostics with that of the Christians. The Gnostics attempted both exorcism and healing but were ineffective in both, while the Christians were successful in rendering these services. Irenaeus went on to say that the Christians did their work without payment and did so with "sympathy, compassion, steadfastness, and truth," in contrast to the performance of the Gnostics. In addition, Irenaeus contended that Christians were able to perform various miracles:

> Wherefore, also, those who are in truth His disciples, receiving grace from Him, do in His name perform [miracles], so as to promote the welfare of other men, according to the gift which each one has received from Him. For some do certainly and truly drive out devils, so that those who have thus been cleansed from evil spirits frequently both believe [in Christ], and join themselves to the Church (Haer.2.32.4).

Irenaeus' phrase "drive out devils" is closer to that of the New Testament than it is to that of Justin, but the testimony is the same. Additionally, the work of casting out demons seemed to result in conversions, thus furthering the evangelical mission of the Church.

In the same chapter, Haer.2.32.5, Irenaeus contrasted the ministry of the Church with that of the occult oriented Gnostics:

> Nor does she perform anything by means of angelic invocations, or by any other wicked curious art; but, directing her prayers to the Lord, who made all things, in a pure, sincere, and straightforward spirit, and calling upon the name of our Lord Jesus Christ, she has been accustomed to work miracles for the advantage of mankind, and not to lead them into error.

Well into the second century, then, Christians were engaged in casting out demons. Their means of doing so was based on the biblical pattern established by Jesus and did not resemble what it would become toward the end of the third century—something quite close to if not identical with pagan exorcisms. That the driving out of devils was effectual is testified to by both Justin and Irenaeus.

Others, such as Tertullian (160-230) and Origin (185-254), also affirm that Christians in their era did cast out, or more correctly, exorcize demons. The point under consideration should be clear: Christians after the era of the New Testament did continue to engage in the casting out of demons and did so in close conformity with the practice as we see it in the New Testament.

Toward the middle of the third century, Church leaders established the office of exorcist. These exorcists were ordained priests, and rites were developed for their use in the practice of exorcism, although exorcism was not among the sacraments. In a matter of little more than two centuries, casting out of demons was ritualized and made the sole propriety of ordained clergy.

CONCLUDING SUMMARY

Although the references to casting out of demons is not abundant in the accounts we have of the Church in the first few centuries, still there are enough notations to affirm that the general Christian community was both aware of casting out of demons and did engage in it. After the mid-third century and the development of the office of exorcist, there was a gradual de-evolution of the ministry into something very akin to that of the pagan exorcist, who relied on incantations, rites, ceremonies, and other magical formulations, even "in the name of Jesus." "Exorcism" became the word most commonly used by the Church in the late third century and beyond for the casting out of demons and was often associated with baptism—as it is today in the Roman Catholic Church.

The practice of casting out demons, or exorcism, continues in all the major branches of Christianity—Eastern Orthodox, Roman Catholic, and the Protestant Churches. To this day, Christians around the world engage in the casting out of demons.

*This chapter owes much to Graham H. Twelftree's book *In the Name of Jesus*. The focus of this fine book is exorcism among early Christians. It was published in 2007 by Baker Academic, Grand Rapids, Michigan.

A Mighty fortress is our god,
A bulwark never failing;
Our helper He amid the flood
Of mortal ills prevailing.
For still our ancient foe
Doth seek to work us woe--
His craft and power are great,
And armed with cruel hate,
On earth is not his equal.

Martin Luther,
"A Mighty Fortress is Our God"
Verse 1

CHAPTER FOUR

A THEOLOGY OF THE DEMONIC

S ince a full or even modest theology of the demonic is beyond the scope of this small book, the following is a mere summary of its most salient points.

THE SERPENT IN THE GARDEN

We begin with Genesis and the serpent in the garden. "Now the serpent was more crafty than any other beast of the field that the LORD God made" (Genesis 3:1).

God, it is clear, made the serpent and gave him certain characteristics. The serpent was crafty—it could reason, communicate, debate, persuade, convince, lie, and deceive. The serpent turned against his creator, however, and God's pronouncement of judgment was, "I will put enmity between you and the woman, and between your offspring and her offspring; he shall bruise your head, and you shall bruise his heel" (Genesis 3:15).

This verse, sometimes regarded as the first prophecy of the Messiah in Scripture, announces that there will be an ongoing war between the serpent and both "the woman" and her "offspring." The woman's offspring has been variously understood as either the Church or Christ or perhaps both.

The offspring of the serpent, in its broadest sense, would include the entire demonic kingdom composed of demons commanded by king Satan. The serpent will do some damage—"bruise his heel," which is not a fatal injury—but the woman's offspring will deliver a mortal blow.

WHO IS THE SERPENT?

Is the serpent Satan? There are a few clues. One is found in 2 Corinthians 11:3: "But I am afraid that as the serpent deceived Eve by his cunning, your thoughts will be led astray from a sincere and pure devotion to Christ." Paul is referring to the serpent of Genesis 3. It is not possible here and now to show how the links between the serpent of Genesis and Satan developed over the centuries, but by Paul's time and with his education under Gamaliel in the school of Hillel he would have identified the serpent with Satan. John made the identification clear in Revelation 12:9:

> And the great dragon was thrown down, that ancient serpent, who is called the devil and Satan, the deceiver of the whole world—he was thrown down to the earth, and his angels were thrown down with him.

Then in Revelation 20:1-3, John continues on the same theme:

> Then I saw an angel coming down from heaven, holding in his hand the key to the bottomless pit and a great chain. And he seized the dragon, that ancient serpent, who is the devil and Satan, and bound him for a thousand years, and threw him into the pit, and shut it and sealed it over him, so that he might not deceive the nations any longer, until the thousand years were ended. After that he must be released for

a little while.

The devil's name is Satan, meaning adversary, opponent, or enemy; Satan wars against God and His creation. The word "devil" is best understood as slanderer or accuser. He was thrown down, which we will consider shortly, but specifically was thrown down to the earth along with his angels. Peter likewise warned, "Your adversary the devil prowls around like a roaring lion, seeking someone to devour" (1 Peter 5:8).

The angels of Revelation 12:9, along with their leader-angel Satan, are created, intelligent beings who have a measure of free will, demonstrated by their capacity to rebel against their creator. How many angels there are, either those who followed Satan or those who did not, is unknown. It is common Christian lore that Satan is one of three archangels, the others being Michael and Gabriel. Satan then seduced the angels under his command—one third of the angelic corps—and they were cast out of heaven along with him. The demonic kingdom is therefore composed of Satan and his angels, his angels being demons, also called evil spirits or unclean spirits.

There is a wide divergence among Christians about the meaning of Revelation 20:1-3, and a clarification of the debate between differing theological systems is not relevant to our purpose here, except to point out that the passage appears to signify that Satan is defeated, which is how any deliverance ministry or casting out of demons is even possible. Without Jesus and His triumph over the devil (see 1 John 3:8), casting out of demons is merely occultic exorcism, a sham casting out of Satan by the power of Satan. The binding of Satan for one thousand years is mysterious; however, Jesus did bind the strong man Satan, when He cast out demons (see Matthew 12:29). It is this binding of Satan that renders him vulnerable to being cast out today.

A PROPHECY OF ISAIAH

Satan is a creature, cast out or thrown down out of heaven, a place outside of time and space in which God dwells. Satan inhabited it in the beginning. The prophet Isaiah provides a mere glimpse into something we cannot possibly imagine:

> How you are fallen from heaven, O Day Star, son of Dawn! How you are cut down to the ground, you who laid the nations low! You said in your heart, 'I will ascend to heaven, above the stars of God I will set my throne on high; I will sit on the mount of assembly in the far reaches of the north; I will ascend above the heights of the clouds; I will make myself like the Most High.' But you are brought down to Sheol, to the far reaches of the pit (Isaiah 14:12-15).

These verses are part of a longer passage, Isaiah 14:3-23, whose context is a pronouncement of judgment upon a king of Babylon. But like so many prophecies in the Hebrew Bible, there suddenly appears something else, something out of context that indicates a shift of the Author's intent. Beginning in verse 12, it is Day Star or Lucifer who is the subject, not a king of Babylon. This is a conclusion, because the prophet does not make a clear identification; but there is a rich history of interpretation of the passage that suggests Isaiah takes the then traditional account of the origins of Satan and applies it to an earthly king.

We know from Genesis 3 that Satan was a heavenly being of some kind, perhaps one of the chief angels. He was created, having a beginning, and he was given freedom of choice. Then something caused Lucifer, who had the exalted titles of Day Star and Son of Dawn, to rebel against God. The consequence was his being cast down to the earth (combining Isaiah and Revelation). And we humans have had to live with this ever after.

A PROPHECY OF EZEKIEL

Isaiah prophesied about a king of Babylon wherein there appeared something that suggests he had more in mind than an earthly king. The same is true with Ezekiel and his prophecy about a king of Tyre:

> Moreover, the word of the LORD came to me: "Son of man, raise a lamentation over the king of Tyre and say to him, Thus says the Lord God: You were the signet of perfection, full of wisdom and perfect in beauty. You were in Eden, the garden of God; every precious stone was your covering" (Ezekiel 28:11-13).

The connection to Satan and the garden is obvious. Except in poetic license was the king of Type ever in Eden. And "full of wisdom and perfect in beauty" could be prophetic hyperbole, but maybe not. Ezekiel's king is like Isaiah's—though so very high and powerful, he falls so very low. Satan is a magnificent creature—wise, beautiful, perfect, murderous, hateful, and deceitful—the ultimate liar and enemy.

DEMONS AND THE NEW TESTAMENT

Two New Testament passages sometimes used to depict an origin for demons are 2 Peter 2:4 and Jude 6:

> For if God did not spare angels when they sinned, but cast them into hell and committed them to chains of gloomy darkness to be kept until the judgment (2

Peter 2:4). And the angels who did not stay within their own position of authority, but left their proper dwelling, he has kept in eternal chains under gloomy darkness until the judgment of the great day (Jude 6).

In these passages the angels are demons, and they made the ultimate mistake and were cast into the lowest and the worst place—hell itself. But if they were cast into hell, how then are they roaming about now? This is an apparent problem with 1 Peter 2:4 and Jude 6. While the identification of fallen angels with demons is not a great leap, it appears that once they had been cast out of heaven the demons are in hell, the place of gloomy darkness, right where they are ready to be employed by the devil for his business. To restate then: hell is not now closed and the demons are not shut up in chains, which they will be upon the return of Jesus Christ at the end of the age.

Finally, we have something Jesus said while speaking of the final judgment: "Then he will say to those on his left, 'Depart from me, you cursed, into the eternal fire prepared for the devil and his angels'" (Matthew 25:41). While 2 Peter 2:4 and Jude 6 speak of a present chaining of demons, Jesus points to a future imprisonment. How this can be reconciled is hard to know, but Jesus said "the devil and his angels," so it is reasonable to think that He meant what He said.

CONCLUDING REMARKS

A significant portion of the Christian worldview holds that God is creator, that He created Satan and the demons who followed him, that God judged sin and Satan, limited their existence, and fixed their destruction, all through the person and work of our Lord Jesus Christ. These great truths are the foundation upon which demons are cast out.

CHAPTER FIVE

HOW PEOPLE ARE INDWELT BY DEMONS

I t is a mystery how people are indwelt by demons, since Scripture is not definite on the subject. The following is based primarily on personal experience.

During the Jesus Movement, many Christians across the country were engaged in casting out demons, which we normally termed "deliverance ministry," based primarily on the phrase from the Lord's Prayer, "Deliver us from evil" (see Matthew 6:13). This ministry became a common topic of conversation during that period. There were those who had a position that casting out of demons was something that belonged strictly to the days of the early Church, and others avoided the ministry all together, believing that it is not possible for Christians to have demons. Many of us who engaged in deliverance ministry compared notes and found a surprising uniformity of experiences. A common understanding of casting out demons emerged, some of which I yet embrace, and some of which I now reject. The common understanding I appeal to now is not science, and probably cannot be tested to meet empirical scientific criteria.

My experience leads me to point to occult practices, mindlessness, and certain religious practices, especially involvement with idols, as the chief means by which people deliberately or inadvertently open themselves up to indwelling spirits.

THE OCCULT

Occult practices may be broken down into three categories: fortune telling, magic (which would include sorcery and witchcraft), and spiritualism (or spiritism). Fortune telling may have many faces, among which are astrology, palm reading, the consulting of psychics who claim to know the future, interpretation of omens, reading the tarot, manipulating a rod and pendulum, crystal gazing, psychometry, playing the ouija board, and many other forms of divination. The central dynamic is a desire to know the future and therefore acquire power.

Magic also has many faces. It may be divided into white, neutral or natural, and black magic. At the end of the spectrum is Satan worship. Magic is an attempt to manipulate gods, celestial beings, guide spirits, ascended masters, forces, energies, angels, demons, and so on, to do one's bidding. The healing or therapeutic touch is a form of magic built on Hindu concepts of energy flow and chakras, which is quite popular today. Periodically, forms of magic will actually enter a culture's mainstream, and few recognize the fundamental magical principles behind them.

Spiritualism's most common form is the séance, or necromancy, which is the attempt to contact the dead. The medium or psychic goes into a trance, becoming, as is supposed, a conduit for a spirit who communicates messages. Such practices are common to religions such as shamanism, Santería, and neo-pagan practices such as Wicca. For a fuller treatment of this consult *The Soul Journey: How Shamanism, Santeria, Wicca, and Charisma are Connected*, by Kent and Katie Philpott, available at www.evpbooks.com.

The Scripture does give a rather comprehensive list of occult practices:

> When you come into the land that the LORD your God is giving you, you shall not learn to follow the abominable practices of those nations. There shall not be found among you anyone who burns his son or his daughter as an offering, anyone who practices divination or tells fortunes or interprets omens, or a sorcerer or a charmer or a medium or a wizard or a necromancer, for whoever does these things is an abomination to the LORD. And because of these abominations the LORD your God is driving them out before you. You shall be blameless before the LORD your God, for these nations, which you are about to dispossess, listen to fortune-tellers and to diviners. But as for you, the LORD your God has not allowed you to do this (Deuteronomy 18:9-14).

Additionally, in the Old Testament there are other references to occult practices. In these passages the King James Version of the Bible used the phrase "familiar spirit(s)" to describe mediums, fortune tellers, and magicians: Leviticus 19:31, 20:6, 20:27; 1 Samuel 28:3-9; 2 Kings 21:6, 23:24; 1 Chronicles 10:13; 2 Chronicles 33:6; Isaiah 8:19, 19:3, and 29:4. The origin of "familiar spirits" is obscure, but it may have been meant to convey the idea that the mediums and fortune tellers knew the identity of the spirit indwelling them, or that the spirit presented itself as the presence of a deceased family member.

The occult is real—that is, it is not entirely smoke and mirrors. Those who have involved themselves in these areas often find that they are in touch with entities or beings that are indeed supernatural. It is quite convincing; and unless someone understands that, however real and powerful, even helpful, these practices are, they are nevertheless unholy and dangerous.

My view then is that by participating in activities that are empowered by the demonic, a person enters, however unwittingly, into Satan's sphere and is vulnerable to invasion.

Jesus promised that where two or three gather in His name, or because of Him, He is present. The exact counterfeit exists in the occult world. When people engage in Satan's religion, then he is present as well. In addition, the counterfeit extends even further. Upon conversion, a person is indwelt by the Holy Spirit of God and becomes a temple of the Spirit. The indwelling of a person by an unholy spirit is the counterfeit, evil opposite of the working of the Holy Spirit. And every spiritual gift, as listed in Romans 12 and 1 Corinthians 12, has its demonic counterfeit.

Often those who engage in occult practices actually seek to be indwelt by guide spirits, angels, energies, celestial beings, and so on, and they are indwelt, but that which indwells them is a demon or demons.

MINDLESSNESS

Mindlessness means a deliberate attempt to empty the mind of all conscious thought. This is a hallmark of some religions, particularly forms of Buddhism and Hinduism. Meditation, where the goal is to empty the mind in order to achieve peace, centeredness, spiritual balance, absence of suffering or passion, oneness with the universe, and so on, exposes the mind and body to invasion by spirits who, seeing the normal protective walls of the mind taken down, come in and fill the empty space. Despite its origins in the above religions, these practices are becoming ever more popular in mainstream western cultures.

Though not entirely to the point, a story Jesus told bears some weight on this issue:

> "When the unclean spirit has gone out of a person, it passes through waterless places seeking rest, but finds none. Then it says, 'I will return to my house from which I came.' And when it comes, it finds the house empty, swept, and put in order. Then it goes and brings with it seven other spirits more evil than itself, and they enter and dwell there, and the last state of that person is worse than the first. So also will it be with this evil generation" (Matthew 12:43-45).

The empty mind, or the mind numbed by extended periods of chanting designed to achieve a kind of mindlessness or cessation of conscious thought, exposes one to the demonic. Synonyms for mindlessness are the passive state of mind, altered state of consciousness, the shamanistic state of mind, trance, and ecstasy. The shaman enters into a trance and goes on a "soul journey" to heaven or hell. Wiccans enter into a trance in order to go on their soul journeys. Even some forms of Christian mysticism rely on trance states to contact superior spiritual planes.

Let it be noted that biblical prayer and meditation is conscious and focused on God Himself or His word or His work. It is far from mindlessness or blanking out of the mind.

THE DEMON BEHIND THE IDOL

A third way that experience has shown me that demons will indwell people is by sacrificing to or making offerings to idols.

Preceding the Jesus People Movement was the explosion of interest in eastern religious teachings. A typical practice of some of these was the making of sacrifices to images and idols representing the religion's gods or to the likeness or picture of a chief or founding guru. Sometimes a mantra or other special name or word was given to a devotee at an initiation ceremony, which was tantamount to an invitation for the spirit of the guru, or the god, or some other spiritual entity, to come into the devotee. Once understood, it became evident that some mantras were literally words of praise to a demon.

That was my experience. And yes, during those years it was not uncommon to cast out from a person a demon disguised as a guru. Paul, writing to a people who lived amongst idol worshippers, said, "flee from idolatry" (1 Corinthians 10:14). He went on to explain:

> What do I imply then? That food offered to idols is anything, or that an idol is anything? No, I imply that what pagans sacrifice they offer to demons and not to God. I do not want you to be participants with demons (1 Corinthians 10:19-20).

When a demon entered the person, a profound spiritual experience might have occurred, which brought some consolation and exhilaration. But over time, as usual, the spiritual presence would turn ugly and begin a tormenting process. Oddly, some of these people would begin to trust in Christ as a result and seek to find relief. Some of them would find that there was relief and deliverance only in Jesus Christ.

TRAUMATIC EXPERIENCES

In recent years I have found that early, mostly childhood experiences involving certain traumas resulted in demonization. Chief among such trauma is fear, abandonment, severe psychical injury, dissolution of family due to deaths, and more. Formerly, I had regarded reactions to these various forms of severe traumatic stress merely from a psychological perspective, but I have recently been forced to re-evaluate my position due to circumstances. Although I have no science and only limited experience to call on, my current view is that traumatic experiences, especially during childhood, are possible mechanisms that lead to demonization.

CONCLUDING REMARKS

To expand on the previous paragraph, some writers will point to other avenues of invasion by demons, such as traumatic emotional experiences such as fear, anger, or rage. Additionally, the use of drugs and other substances such as psychedelics, including marijuana, may expose one to demons. Though this is not as clear as occult practices, it should not be ruled out. Anything that takes one substantially out of his mind has the potential for trouble. However, there does not appear to be any concern with the medical procedural use of anesthetics. This is a murky area, so probably the less said the better. It is not necessary to know how demonic invasion took place but rather how to know if they are present and, if so, how to cast them out.

A point of emphasis: demons will entertain, assist, please, comfort, and otherwise seem to benefit those whom they indwell. A demon will become a "close" friend with its host. The ultimate intention of a demon is to destroy God's creation and to separate the person it indwells from God forever. The demon will use whatever means necessary to achieve that goal. Suicide is the final solution; that is, the demon aims to drive a person to suicide. This does not mean that every suicide is demonically inspired—no, not at all. However, once dead, a person's eternal destiny is forever fixed.

See an expansion of the discussion of how people are indwelt by demons in chapter 9 of this new edition. Some things will be re-stated and new material is added.

DID WE IN OUR OWN STRENGTH CONFIDE,
OUR STRIVING WOULD BE LOSING,
WERE NOT THE RIGHT MAN ON OUR SIDE,
THE MAN OF GOD'S OWN CHOOSING.
DOST ASK WHO THAT MAY BE?
CHRIST JESUS, IT IS HE--
LORD SABAOTH HIS NAME,
FROM AGE TO AGE THE SAME,
AND HE MUST WIN THE BATTLE.

MARTIN LUTHER,
"A MIGHTY FORTRESS IS OUR GOD"
VERSE 2

CHAPTER SIX

CAN CHRISTIANS HAVE DEMONS?

There is no clear consensus on this issue among Bible-believing Christians. It is agreed that Christians can be influenced by demons, as in oppression or deception, but regarding demonization or possession, there is sometimes sharp disagreement.

I have held both positions, and while I currently hold that Christians can be indwelt by demons, it is not clear to me how this can happen. My theology is that in Christ we are a new creation; the old has passed away and the new has come. Furthermore, we are made holy in Christ, our sin is covered and forgiven, we are indwelt by the Holy Spirit, placed into the Body of Christ, and even seated with Christ at the right hand of the Father in heaven. How can a demon possibly remain in a Christian, even if there was one present prior to conversion?

If we use the common analogy of a liquid-filled glass that has no room to accept a new liquid, we suggest that being filled with the Holy Spirit makes us incapable of simultaneously being filled with an unclean spirit. Of course this is human logic and may not apply to the issue before us.

BIBLICAL SUPPORT?

Logical systems of theology tend to maintain a position against a Christian having an indwelling unclean spirit. However, is there any biblical support for this? One passage that may speak to the issue is Acts 5:1-3:

> But a man named Ananias, with his wife Sapphira, sold a piece of property, and with his wife's knowledge he kept back for himself some of the proceeds and brought only a part of it and laid it at the apostles' feet. But Peter said, "Ananias, why has Satan filled your heart to lie to the Holy Spirit and to keep back for yourself part of the proceeds of the land?"

Satan filled Ananias' heart. Does this mean that a demon had been indwelling him all along? Is there positive proof that Ananias was definitely born again of the Spirit of God? Was Ananias demonized or merely deceived without the presence of an indwelling unclean spirit? These questions cloud the issue to the point that it cannot be said one way or another whether Ananias had an indwelling demon or not.

MY EXPERIENCE

My experience, for whatever it is worth, is that it is usually only Christians who will actually want to go through the process of having demons cast out. It is very rare for a non-Christian to submit to this; they will suffer torment by demons, often knowing the source of the torment to be demons, yet they will be loath to lose some perceived benefit from the demons and will often finally choose not to suffer the loss, as strange as that may seem. This is not an unusual occurrence.

Christians who have sought deliverance will have, at some point, realized there is something wrong in their lives, and despite applying the disciplines of the normal Christian life, find there is yet a resistance, a barrier that is neither emotional in nature nor a form of rebellion—these are the ones who seek help. If deliverance ministry is available, it is rather quick and simple to see if an indwelling demon is indeed present. If there is, then that can be dealt with. If there is not, then other forms of ministry and care are required.

IS IT A MOOT POINT?

How certain are we that a person is actually born again? When I look back on the years when there was a great demand for the casting out of demons and remember individual cases, I sometimes wonder whether I was dealing with a person who was a Christian or one who was merely christianized. I have no answer, but my experience over the years has taught me that not everyone who says, "Lord, Lord" is truly a born-again believer.

My point is not to let any dogmatic theology that has no clear biblical warrant determine whether I extend ministry to someone who comes for help, especially in an area with so much uncertainty. I will not turn anyone away who seeks Jesus for freedom and peace.

And though this world, with devils filled,
Should threaten to undo us,
We will not fear, for God hath willed
His truth to triumph through us.
The prince of darkness grim,
We tremble not for him--
His rage we can endure,
For lo, his doom is sure:
One little word shall fell him.

Martin Luther,
"A Mighty Fortress is Our God"
Verse 3

CHAPTER SEVEN

HOW TO CAST OUT DEMONS

One can hardly fault the person who considers this whole business of Satan and demons to be ludicrous and judges the proponents of deliverance ministry to be either misguided or arrogant. It has not been an easy decision to once again bring attention to this realm of the supernatural and the need for Christians to take this work seriously. If it were not for the fact that Jesus cast out demons, the apostles cast out demons, Philip and Paul and the unknown disciple and others down through the ages cast out demons, and Christians like me cast out demons in modern times, it would be tempting to ignore the whole thing. My driving concern is for those who are chained by demonic spirits and for those who would attempt to bring deliverance to those tormented by unclean spirits.

CAUTIONS

It is not a good practice to seek out people whom one might think have a demon and offer to cast it out. Jesus did not do this; usually the demonized person was brought to Jesus, or Jesus came upon a demonized person in His travels. It is best that a person understands that he or she is coming to Jesus for His healing ministry. Early on I did not know this was the proper protocol, and on one or two occasions I did pay the price for my ignorance. The service of casting out of demons is not to be advertised or promoted; God will bring whom He will to those who are ready and equipped to do this ministry.

Certain proprietary measures must be observed also. It is not wise for one person to do the work of casting out demons unaccompanied. I have done it, but only out of necessity. Two Christians is preferred. If a woman is the recipient of the ministry, it is absolutely necessary that a woman minister be present.

I do not recommend that deliverance ministry be conducted with minors, even with parental consent or even with parents being present. In the 1960s and 1970s I did not give this issue a thought, but now it is far different. Yes, children can become demonized, especially by means of traumatic events; it is best to educate parents on how to do the work. But even here parents run the risk of being accused of child abuse. I wish I had something more helpful to say on this particular issue, but I do not.

JESUS WITH US

Is it possible to bring someone to Jesus in our day? It would seem so. When two or more of us gather for something having to do with prayer, praise, worship, preaching, fellowship, or even church discipline, which is the context of the Matthew 18:20 promise of Jesus, then Jesus is present. This is His own promise.

When we gather to bring Christian ministry to someone who has requested this, then we have the confidence that Jesus is with us. It is not required that the subjects of the ministry visualize Jesus or imagine Him being present in his or her mind. No, this is not a mind game; it is reliance upon our Lord Jesus Christ to do the work He has called us to.

A KEY VERSE

SUBMIT YOURSELVES THEREFORE TO GOD. RESIST THE DEVIL, AND HE WILL FLEE FROM YOU. (JAMES 4:7)

This one verse is the heart of the ministry of casting out of demons. "Submit" must include reliance upon God as opposed to anyone or anything else. Submit to, trust in, rely upon, commit to—all have to do with a relationship with God who casts out demons, who alone has the power and authority to command demons to obey. "Resist" is a decided stance against cooperation with the demonic, refusing to listen to the deceiving voice, being resolute in the desire to be out from underneath the dictates of the evil one. Following the admonishment to submit and resist is the promise that the devil will flee. The demon flees from the presence of the Holy One of Israel, the Lord Jesus Christ.

HOW DO WE KNOW IF SOMEONE HAS A DEMON OR NOT?

In most instances, it will not be known by someone other than the indwelt person whether he or she definitely has a demon. More often, it is only the indwelt person who knows of the presence of a demon, or that person may wonder if or suspect that a demon is present. The charismatic gift of "the ability to distinguish between spirits" of 1 Corinthians 12:10 may be rare, and during the years when I thought I had this gift, I was frequently wrong.

It is not necessary to know if someone has a demon. Commonly, we pray with a person and simply begin to cast out any demons that might be indwelling a person. This may take some time, because there may be no response for some period. But if a demon is present, it will begin to show itself. This showing of itself is not easily described. Generally, a demon will take over the person, to some degree, and begin contorting the person's face and speaking through the person, using the person's vocal cords. It is something easily observed and usually quite apparent.

A demon may not show up in a timely fashion. On one occasion, a minister partner of mine and I prayed for nearly two months, once per week for one to two hours per session, and decided there was no demon present at all. The parents who had brought the young woman to us (the father was pastor of a church and was certain something had happened to his daughter) were convinced that we should continue, despite the fact that no demons seemed to be involved. Finally, however, the decision was made to end the ministry after one last effort. Again, after a lengthy prayer period, we concluded that no deliverance ministry was necessary. The young woman's father then celebrated communion with us, and as his daughter was about to drink of the Cup of the Lord, she fell down in a seeming faint. My friend and I knelt down beside her, and in just a few minutes time, several demons were cast out of her. And this was after many previous long hours of ordering the demons to come out in the name of Jesus.

Some demons manifest quickly, and others do not. This is one of the reasons I never enjoyed this service, because it could take many hours of real work. Usually, however, when a person is submitting to God, is relying on Jesus to cast out demons, and is resisting Satan, the work will go fairly quickly.

THE ACTUAL GATHERING

It is best to meet in a place where any loud screams will not bring the police, which has happened to me. On that occasion I simply explained what was going on, and that was sufficient for the officer. But do not count on this.

It is also best to meet with two or more people who have some experience with casting out demons. If this is not possible, then older and more mature believers would be the ideal. Remember, this is not a ritualized ministry. It is largely prayer and commanding demons to come out.

Generally, if circumstances permit, I like to begin with a rehearsal of the reason for the gathering. This makes things clear and gives the person to whom we are ministering an opportunity to ask questions. Then I remind people of the victory of Jesus over the demonic kingdom, often reading a verse or two, then go into prayer, asking our almighty God to glorify Himself in this ministry. Some of the verses I like to refer to are James 4:7; 1 John 3:8; Luke 9:1-2; I John 4:4; Romans 8:31-39; Ephesians 6:12-18; and Colossians 2:13-15, with many more as possibilities.

On several occasions it has happened that during an initial prayer I have suddenly looked up to find the subject of the ministry hovering over me in a menacing manner. Quite unnerving!

After an initial prayer and the general orientation, I turn to the individual and command a demon to come out. Just like that—with no fanfare or anything else—I begin to command a demon to come out.

Very often, this is a point when a demon manifests itself. It is right there in the person, so that now we are dealing with the demon and not the person. The demon uses the body of the person—this is what is meant by "manifest itself." It might use the vocal cords; contort the body, especially the face; it might swear, scream, cause the person to go into a kind of swoon, cough, vomit; or, most commonly, begin to argue with the ministers. The argument may focus on the ability of the ministers to cast out the demon, or that it is better for one reason or another for the demon to remain. Demons have a highly tuned intelligence and are good at debate. Debate, however, should not be allowed. It took some time for me to understand this.

During the course of the ministry or time of prayer and commanding a demon to leave, it is as though the person had been submerged, and now the demon is prominent. This can be rather frightening at first; and it can become confusing as to whom is being encountered, the demon or the person. At the end of a deliverance session, during a kind of de-briefing, I have found that a person would remember little if anything of the events taking place during the session. I am not sure what this means.

There have been a number of times when I have been attacked by the person under the influence of the demon. Blows to the face, fingers around my neck, being kicked, and other physical unpleasantness, but without a resulting mark or bruise. And I do not touch the person unless I have to. I will admit to having engaged, though not of my own choosing, in wrestling matches. This is definitely not recommended, and such events are evidence that there must be a regrouping, with more prayer and counseling preceding any new attempt. Those who have seen such physical assaults are usually amazed, as I usually am also. Through it all, I have never been actually hurt, although there have been times that the demonic manifestation has shaken me, making it necessary to compose myself.

One lesson learned in this ministry is that demons are weak, despite the huffing and the puffing. They may roar initially, screaming awful things, even making horrendous movements, and then come out with a whimper. At the beginning, a demon may rage and scream defiance, while at the end, just before the demon is expelled, it pleads not to be cast out, and the last pleas sound like a little child crying for help.

A deliverance session may be lengthy; often it has been

necessary to assure a person that the work will continue until the demons are gone. A number of times I have thought this ministry is a young man's work, and I never look forward to it now in my seventies, since it can be exhausting. The problem is that demons will often refuse to do what they are commanded to do, and why they do not, I do not understand. It may be that the person is not ready for the demons to leave or has not submitted and resisted in accordance with James 4:7. It is not necessary to understand everything.

Often, when I become tired, I stop and begin to talk about what the individual is experiencing. The person is usually in considerable discomfort, but not always, and I have found it more productive, if the discomfort is present. There may well be a conversation going on with a demon in the mind of the person. Demons do something for an individual—perform something desirable. The demon will inform the person that the goodies will all stop once it is cast out. Now, this may seem ludicrous, but is it very common. It is the Faustian trade, a giving of the soul for something of value, and the demon plays on that. Or, the demon may be threatening to kill or somehow do damage to some other person, if it is cast out. Or, the demon threatens to return once the "Christians" leave. Many, many are the devices of demonic spirits, and when the deliverance session is long and drawn out, there is usually a reason, perhaps one I have just mentioned.

In long sessions, I sing hymns, read Scripture, have a time of confessing of sin, or engage in general conversation. In the conversations, important issues may come up. It may be that the person is carrying certain occult items on his or her person or keeps them at home, or there is something else that should be discussed and dealt with. A demon will remind a person of all the awful things he or she has done, and if the session continues, it will shame the person by obnoxious displays or a recitation of the person's past sins. I could go on and on with this, but the point is that a demon will do anything to stay in the person. One is reminded of the legion of demons who wanted to be sent into the pigs. Remember that demons are liars. Many times I have been told that they are gone. Not very clever, of course, for if they were gone they would no longer be talking! Demons will sometimes give conditions for their leaving, usually impossible conditions—anything to remain.

HOW TO KNOW WHEN THE MINISTRY TO AN INDIVIDUAL SHOULD BE CONCLUDED

Deliverance work continues until no more demons manifest themselves. This may take a number of sessions. A dominant demon may leave first or may leave last. It can be tricky, and it is not necessary to know at the outset all the ins and outs. We simply cast out the demons; we do not play games with them. When it is clear that an ending point is reached—either the demons are all gone, or we have grown tired—then an ending prayer is good, thanking God for His grace and power. After a while, the person will learn how to cast his or her demons out alone. I know this sounds strange, but this has been my experience.

ARE DEMONS TO BE CAST INTO HELL?

Where do demons go once they are cast out? There is no solid biblical answer to this question. Jesus allowed the legion of demons to go into pigs, but from there, the Scripture does not fill in the blanks.

It is common for deliverance ministers to make statements such as, "I command you to go to the pit of hell," or "I command you never to return here again," and so on. Whether the deliverance ministers have this warrant is unclear. I do usually say such things, but I am conscious that when I do, it is not entirely biblical. Demons, according to the story Jesus told in Matthew 12:43-45, may return to reoccupy a vacuum. It is essential, therefore, that a person, once delivered from demons, continue to practice the admonition of James 4:7.

TESTING THE SPIRITS

> Beloved, do not believe every spirit, but test the spirits to see whether they are from God, for many false prophets have gone out into the world. By this you know the Spirit of God: every spirit that confesses that Jesus Christ has come in the flesh is from God, and every spirit that does not confess Jesus is not from God. This is the spirit of the antichrist, which you heard was coming and now is in the world already (1 John 4:1-3).

In his letters and Gospel, John did not directly deal with the casting out of demons. It has been a puzzle as to why he left out all incidents of Jesus casting out demons, as opposed to the synoptic Gospel writers. That is another study, and even in this passage it is questionable whether the spirits are demons or people who are denying the incarnation, as did most Gnostics during that era. Perhaps John had in mind that those who denied that God had become flesh were inspired by demons. I raise this issue to prevent a type of confusion that I suffered from in the early days of my deliverance ministry. It is best explained by quoting James 2:19: "You believe that God is one; you do well. Even the demons believe—and shudder."

Demons know who Jesus is—they know He is the Holy One of Israel and that He has come to destroy them (see Mark 1:21-27 and Matthew 8:28-34). Demons have a rather sound theology; they do know who God is, and they shudder. They are even able to say, "Jesus is Lord," "I believe in Jesus," "I believe Jesus came in the flesh," "I want to be saved," "I will follow Jesus," and so on. Does this sound strange? It might, except that we know Satan is a liar and a deceiver. It is one thing to say something and another to live it. All believing is not equal. Biblical faith is given by God and is far more than anything human beings can come to themselves. Demons cannot have saving faith in Jesus; they cannot be saved, converted, or forgiven. The unclean spirits and Satan, their leader, are under the judgment and condemnation of God. There is no repentance for these—no forgiveness, no second chance. I say this, because I have known people who thought otherwise and actually directed much of their supposed evangelistic ministry toward demons. This always ended badly.

SOLITARY CASTING OUT OF DEMONS

Due to necessity, a person can be taught to cast out demons without anyone else being present. There have been a number of times when people have called from out of state or even from other countries, and there was nothing else to do but give a brief teaching on deliverance and suggest that the person cast out their demons alone. Also, I have attempted to do this over the phone. The results are not verifiable, but people have reported that demons did leave.

KEEPING CONFIDENCE

This ministry should be conducted with the confidence that it will not be talked about with others. Herein is often a problem. Due to the startling and incredible nature of this work, it is talked about, often bragged about, and this is why only older and mature Christians should be involved. I decline to perform this ministry when others want to be in on a deliverance session out of not much more than curiosity. This must not happen.

DANGER?

It is thought that there may be danger involved in casting out demons, especially the fear that those casting out the demons might be indwelt or invaded by the very demons that are being cast out. I have not seen this, nor have I heard of such an event from others who engage in this ministry. Not that it could not happen if an occult type of exorcism instead of biblical casting out of demons is involved. However, this work must not be entered into lightly but taken very seriously. It should never become so commonplace that it is not recognized that it is Satan who is being engaged and that he is a lion roaring about looking for someone to devour. Those who are merely curious should not do the work, nor should a session ever be recorded in any manner, either by video or audio recording.

CAN DEMONS RETURN?

Jesus told a story directly relating to the question of whether a demon can return to re-demonize a person out of whom it has been cast out.

> "When the unclean spirit has gone out of a person, it passes through waterless places seeking rest, but finds none. Then it says, 'I will return to my house from which I came.' And when it comes, it finds the house empty, swept, and put in order. Then it goes and brings with it seven other spirits more evil than itself, and they enter and dwell there, and the last state of that person is worse than the first. So also will it be with this evil generation" (Matthew 12:43-45).

The parallel passage in Luke 11:24-26 lacks the last sentence in Matthew, "So also will it be with this evil generation." There is quite a history of interpretation involved here, with many commentators on the conservative side accepting the factualness of how demons operate, essentially that they can return. It should be pointed out that the context in Matthew's passage has something to do with the religious views of the scribes and Pharisees, which could only result in a religiously observant follower of their teaching being cleaned out but not filled with God's Holy Spirit. It would be counter-productive, even dangerous, for a person who is not indwelt or who would not become indwelt by the Holy Spirit through conversion, to have demons cast out. Without the indwelling Holy Spirit there would be no defense against a re-demonizing. This is an aspect of the argument that having the indwelling of the Holy Spirit is a perfect defense against being invaded by demons or unclean spirits. This generally matches my own experience.

SOMETHING TO KEEP IN MIND

We recall that Jesus told the seventy-two that they should not get excited that the demons were subject to them but glad only that their names were written in heaven. This must be the mindset of those who do the work of casting out of demons.

Those of us who have engaged in the ministry of casting out of demons will be embarrassed about the extremes to which some take this normative ministry. It has become the focus of some groups, often teaching and preaching about it to the exclusion of central ministries, especially the proclamation of the Gospel. Casting out demons must be only one part of the ministry of a church, and there should be no attempt to publicize it. Scripturally, healing and casting out demons were signs that pointed to Jesus and the Kingdom of God.

CHAPTER EIGHT

HEARING VOICES

A fter reading Gail A. Hornstein's *Agnes's Jacket: a Psychologist's Search for the Meaning of Madness* (published by Rodale in 2007), I thought it proper to add this chapter to the new edition.

Dr. Hornstein argues for a new way of looking at and treating those among us who suffer from mental illness. The "biochemical disturbance" paradigm has not been all together effective in treating such conditions as schizophrenia, clinical depression, bi-poplar, and personality disorders, and much of the evidence for this comes from those who had been given a psychiatric diagnosis and treated with medications of one form or another. Much of my own education was in psychology, and for ten years, as a pastor of an evangelical church in San Rafael, California, I unofficially practiced as a therapist. Concurrent with that, I engaged in casting out demons from many hundreds of persons who, of their own free will, came for help and ministry.

Though not sharing Dr. Hornstein's position (she is not writing as a Christian therapist or theologian), I found myself agreeing with some of her positions. Many of those who had been institutionalized, sometimes for years, found relief through nothing more than what may be referred to as "talk therapy" and participating in support groups with those of like experience.

HEARING VOICES

What caught my attention more than some of the other valuable insights I found in the book, was the large number of people coming forth with the admission that they hear voices—ones that are not coming from actual people around them but are located somewhere internal to the hearer. Dr. Hornstein described the development and growth of the Hearing Voices Network that, at the time of her writing, was operational mostly in England and Europe. Many of those who participate in this network have neither been institutionalized nor prescribed psychotropic drugs.

I could not help but recall all the people for whom we had prayed to have demons cast out who also routinely heard voices. It was not uncommon to find that while we were praying that Jesus would cast out demons, the subject was in conversation with voices within. And we did not know, and do not know to this day, if the voices in every instance were actual demons or not, but quite often it became abundantly evident that such was the case.

Jesus talked to voices coming from demonized persons. Mark 1:34 is representative of this: "And he healed many who were sick with various diseases, and cast out many demons. And he would not permit the demons to speak, because they knew him."

Let us be clear: I am not saying that mental illness is caused by evil spirits; however, I think that in some cases there is a demonic element involved. And this because after such "voices" were cast out, the voices disappeared and did not return, even when the subject went through stressful periods.

THE TRADE-OFF

Dozens of times, when no demons "manifested" during our deliverance sessions, I would stop the process and ask the subject what was happening or what they were experiencing. And then I would hear the report of what the voices were saying. Typically, it went along these lines: "If I leave, you will be lonely." "I will not give you what you want, if I leave." "I will enter into your wife, husband, child, mother, friend, and so on, if I leave." "You will suffer greatly, and you might even die, if I leave." "You will commit suicide, if I leave." And this accounting is abbreviated. The effect was that there would be a significant loss to the subject, if the demon(s) left. On a number of occasions, the subject called a halt to the deliverance and preferred to have what the demon gave and/or avoid dire consequences if it left. Let me give one example that happened fairly recently.

An athletic, good looking young man in his thirties lived in a high end apartment complex near a popular grocery market. A "person" he regularly talked to in his head would alert him to cross the street to the market, whereupon he would find a young woman in the store wandering through the aisles. He would then be able to present himself and take her across the street to his apartment and have sex with her. This had been going on for years, and over time the voice began to be more and more demanding, would yell and shout at him to the point that it made it difficult for him to function in his Silicon Valley tech firm job. Somehow he heard about me, phoned, and asked if maybe I could help him.

We met on a Saturday afternoon in my office. We talked for some period, maybe an hour or more, as he spoke of what had been happening to him. I acted the therapist, and we discussed his upbringing and traumatic events he had experienced in his life. Finally we got down to business, and

I began to pray and ask Jesus to cast out any demons the subject might have.

He sat still for a long period of time looking as though he were deep in thought. There was none of the usual demonic activity, no obvious spiritual battle underway. After a time I stopped praying and commanding demons to come out and asked him what was going on.

In a very forthright manner he simply said that the voice told him he would not get any more women over to his place for sex if the voice left him. He calmly told me he would rather keep the voice, if the voice was getting him the young women. He walked out of my office, and I have not heard from him since.

It sounds much like the proverbial Faustian trade-off: give me your soul and I will give you____ (whatever it might be). The price is rather steep however— everlasting hell. Momentary pleasure, even if decades in duration, is poor payment for spending eternity at the mercy of the voices.

Just one more story: A middle aged man who never married, had no family, no real friends, and was out of work for a long period lived alone in a residential hotel and rarely interacted with others. He would be seen holding long conversations with someone no one could see. When questioned, and gently so, about this, he reported that he had an ongoing relationship with a voice for a long time. They would spend many hours together every day, and he was no longer lonely.

The subject knew the nature of the voice; he knew it was an evil spirit, since the voice told him who he actually was. He knew what was afoot and understood that the evil spirit could be cast out, but the subject preferred the demon's presence, because he was so fearful of being lonely again.

Let me say that the above two illustrations cover many of the reasons people decline to have demons cast out. It is the immediacy of the comfort, pleasure, or whatever goodie is involved that matters most.

Loneliness has long been part of the human experience. Being alone over a long period of time can trigger emotional distress. This has been observed when prisoners were subjected to what is commonly referred to as solitary confinement. It wears one down. And if one is hearing voices, it is at least some form of comfort.

The following are descriptions of the nature or characteristics of voices drawn from Gail A. Hornstein's *Agnes's Jacket*:

- Voices give advice, threaten, swear, or inspire.
- They tell people to do things they may or may not want to do.
- Voices can be loud and articulate or barely audible.
- They can be accompanied by whispers, mutterings, or humming.
- They can incorporate strange noises—ticking or clicking, bits of melody or the far-off whoosh of a seashell held up to the ear.
- Voices can be male, female, or a mixture of both. It is not always possible to tell the gender of the voices, even after years of hearing them.
- The voices may sound as if they are coming from young children, or they may be robotic and machinelike.
- The voices may sound like someone the person knows now or in the past.
- The voices may sound totally unfamiliar.
- Some people hear voices only in certain contexts. For others, they are a constant presence.
- Some voices speak the person's thoughts out loud, or two or three voices argue or provide a running commentary on the voice hearer's behavior.
- Some voices issue commands.
- Some make threats or repeat a certain word or phrase.
- Voices compel attention—hearing them is too powerful

an experience to be ignored.

- Most voice hearers are confused or frightened, at least at first.
- Some are angered at being singled out.
- Others feel special for having been chosen for such a mystical, otherworldly experience.
- Some will see themselves as a medium or clairvoyant.
- Some will be convinced they are having a breakdown.
- If the voices are commanding or unrelenting, it may ultimately prove too exhausting to resist them.
- Some think voices are spirits—of dead people, demons, angels, or God.
- Some think the voices are telepathic communications from another dimension or from outer space.
- Some agonize that there is something wrong with how their brains function.
- Many voice hearers say their voices appeared early in their lives.
- Some report that they first heard their voices after a trauma (sexual abuse, bereavement, illness, or parental divorce, etc.).
- Most voice hearers learn to cope with the voices while others are overwhelmed.
- Voices hearers think their voices are not their own thinking or a talking to themselves.
- Voices are experienced as coming from other people, from birds or other animals, or from the TV, radio, or other objects.
- Some voice hearers feel tortured by the voices while others welcome them as inspirations or guides to better living.

Now then, when "voices" are demons, they can be withstood and cast out. My approach is usually one of quoting James 4:7, "Submit yourselves therefore to God. Resist the devil, and he will flee from you." Once the subject resists the voices, even orders them to "shut up" and leave, the deliverance will proceed well enough.

Again, it is not clear that voices are always demons. How does one tell the difference? I wish I had some insight on this, but I do not. Voices, if they are not demons, cannot be cast out. Emotional and mental illnesses are not cast out; they can be dealt with, however, and this is where psychologists like Gail Hornstein and programs like Hearing Voices Network come in.

That word above all earthly powers,
No thanks to them, abideth;
The Spirit and the gifts are ours
Through Him who with us sideth.
Let goods and kindred go,
This mortal life also--
The body they may kill;
God's truth abideth still:
His kingdom is forever.

Martin Luther,
"A Mighty Fortress is Our God"
Verse 4

CHAPTER NINE

HOW TO BECOME POSSESSED BY DEMONS

hapter five covers the means of becoming possessed
by demons, and that subject is perhaps the chief reason that many readers will acquire this book. It is a
subject that keeps surfacing and is frankly one I would rather
avoid. In the mid-1970s I co-authored a book that dealt with
the subject, resulting in a flood of people who wanted to
look into the subject more carefully. During that period the
occult largely flew under the radar, but it has now emerged
as mainstream and garners a great deal of attention in all
forms of media, attracting a growing number of people who
honestly want to know more. Therefore, this chapter covers
the issue more thoroughly.

Neo-pagan practices like **Wicca** have swept across the
country, key components of which are magic(k), spiritism,
fortune telling, and more.

Shamanism in many guises is growing in popularity in
the West, with shamans from multiple cultures advertising
their services on the Internet. Here the occult is center stage
and loudly announced.

Santería, one of the largest and fastest growing of the
world's religions, is utterly reliant on occult theory and prac-

tice, from spells and divination to contacting the dead.

Why is this so? One reason is that the occult is spiritual to its core and provides an alternative to humanist materialism. Many a materialist has moved to a spiritual orientation after direct contact with the spirit world. Perhaps an even deeper reason for the popularity of groups that are spiritistic is the quest for power. Since power is the main focus of religions like Wicca, Santería, and various other forms of shamanism, those who feel powerless are strongly tempted to the occult arts.

But there is a problem. Contact and involvement with the occult is a sure and quick route to being possessed by demons. Shocking? For many who succumb to the temptation, the sense that power indwells them is a prized goal. However, the horrific and vile nature of that power within is a realization usually made too late.

The word "possessed" is troublesome, because most people think that a possessed person acts in a crazy or bizarre manner and is constantly under the control of a demonic spirit. Were it that simple! Most possessed persons rarely realize their condition, and it is rarely seen or confirmed by family or friends. The devil prefers to lie low and only slowly, little by little, wreak havoc. People may eventually figure out what has grabbed hold of them, but then they are left wondering what in the world to do. Most of them can only suppress and deny or run and cover, since no one in our culture wants to look like a "mental case." How many of them abuse substances to keep the demons at bay?

WHAT "OPENS THE DOOR" TO POSSESSION?

THE OCCULT
There are three primary divisions in the occult world: for-

tune telling or divination, spiritualism, and magic.

FORTUNE TELLING. This is everything from the Ouija Board to the palm reader, but it includes psychic readings, the I Ching, tea leaf reading, astrology, tarot card reading, and a great many more practices.

SPIRITUALISM OR SPIRITISM. The focus here is the séance, which can take any number of forms but is the attempt to contact the spirits or souls of the dead. It is known from ancient times, is mentioned in the Bible, and is still popular, since actual spirits are contacted.

MAGIC. This is sorcery, witchcraft, and spells and curses, and it is the manipulation of spirits, gods, and goddesses to do one's bidding through the performance of rites and rituals. The world of magic is complicated but far more common than most recognize. Whether white, neutral, or black, magic is still magic. Some of those involved rationalize that they are only invested in good magic or natural magic but not the bad varieties. However, the devil does not pay attention to such distinctions. Magic is magic, and magic is within the devil's realm.

OCCULT INVOLVEMENT

By this I mean giving into, believing in, trusting in, acting on, or relying on, any overt form of occultism, which is more than casual contact. How much is enough to become demon possessed? Who knows, but the devil never plays fairly.

After decades of dealing with people who have attracted and finally become possessed by demons, I have discovered that when people give themselves to the occult, in whatever form it might take, they expose themselves to the possibility of being possessed by evil or unclean spirits, all of which are ruled over by Satan. Satan is not a pleasant house guest.

QUEST FOR POWER AND KNOWLEDGE

These are the central motives that bring people into the

occult world. That power and knowledge is accessed is not to be denied. The Faustian trade-off is operable, however; the devil will give gifts in order to achieve dominance over a person's life.

Satan is a gift giver and is especially good, for a period of time, at providing power, sex, money, and other goodies we humans desire. He gives to get, and this principle must not be underestimated. His assistance comes with strings attached, and he usually yanks back the delights and replaces them with torments, sooner or later.

TRAUMATIC EVENTS

Below is a short list of traumatic events that may open a person up to being invaded by demonic spirits. How this works I do not know, but that it does I have been made painfully aware.

A NEAR-DEATH EXPERIENCE is chief among the traumas that the devil uses to capture unwary and vulnerable prey. People of all ages have spoken of experiences in which they returned from the brink of death or even after actual biological death occurred. They describe being conscious, witnessing a wide assortment of events, and even conversing with people. Some of these "remembered experiences" result in bestselling books or films. It is virtually impossible, however, to fact-check the reports on what occurs in the brain of someone during this process. It is likely that the complex electrical and chemical mix that goes to work on the central nervous system of one who is on the brink of death produces incredible hallucinations.

A FRIGHTENING EXPERIENCE, such as being in an automobile accident, being lost in the woods, accosted by strangers intent on great bodily harm, even seeing gruesome and horrific acts, even on film or television, often produces lingering fear that can make one vulnerable.

SEXUAL MOLESTATION when a child has been known to result in not only significant emotional distress that may last for many years but can also open a person up to demonization. Encountering this circumstance in deliverance ministry is not a pleasant experience, and exploration of it should only be attempted with great caution and counsel from professionals.

A DEATH IN THE FAMILY may trigger unwanted visitations from spiritual entities or produce dreams and visions that are of an unusual nature. The devil will take advantage of emotional vulnerability in times of grief and distress. To suddenly encounter the spirit world is life changing to all who experience it. Books and movies about such experiences continue to emerge, from both Christian and secular publishers and filmmakers, and this makes me rather suspicious. The story lines are nearly always the same: the dearly departed always communicate that they are okay and have landed in a good place after death. This is one of the devil's favorite plot twists.

Linked to the discussion of near-death experiences above is what happens in the lives of the newly bereaved. Reflecting on my four-plus decades as a pastor, during which I conducted several hundred memorial and funeral services, I recall frequent episodes of demonic activity played out in the lives of those whose loved ones had died. Perhaps it is an appearance of the departed in a dream or even while fully awake. At a time of loss we are thrown off emotionally and will imagine things we would not otherwise consider, and this is not necessarily of a Satanic nature. That said, it is nevertheless true that the devil knows all too well that grieving people are vulnerable to deception.

INITIATIONS INTO RELIGIONS

As a part of the initiation into some religions, the initiate may be required to make an invitation to be indwelt by a dead guru, some other spiritual entity such as a god or goddess, or even the devil himself.

SATANISM is a religion, and the introduction into it is a deliberate inviting of Satan to take control over one's life, whether through a focused worship of the devil as god or reliance upon a "spirit" for guidance. The attraction toward devil worship is powerful and lustful, an almost irresistible lure from which few can escape once they are trapped.

When devotees of TRANSCENDENTAL MEDITATION and KRISHNA CONSCIOUSNESS undergo initiation ceremonies, they are knowingly inviting the spirit of a dead guru to inhabit their minds and bodies. Of course, a demon shows up instead, but the devotee does not realize that he or she has been duped. The power gurus like Muktananda and Rajneesh had their "spirits" within them, and as submission was made to the guru, it was in fact a submission to evil spirits. Current gurus continue in a similar mode.

In the asiento or initiation into SANTERÍA, the initiate is essentially "mounted" or possessed by an orisha deity. Here the possession is deliberate; the deception is that instead of the expected god or goddess, what possesses the head of the initiate is a demonic spirit.

What are the animal guides or spirits that WICCANS meet on their soul journeys? They are certainly demonic spirits in disguise. The elves and fairies are cute; gnomes are curious looking; animal helpers are intriguing or majestic; goddesses may be clothed in spectacular auras; Zeus, Diana, Apollo, Moses, Abraham, Elijah, angels Gabriel and Raphael may dazzle; and John the Baptist, Jesus, Peter, and Paul may seem to appear with special messages and prophecies. They are all merely familiar spirits who are expert in disguise, even down to the molecular level, but are no more than demons (see 2 Corinthians 11:14-15).

THE TRANCE STATE

The trance state (or the ecstasy, passive state of mind, altered state of consciousness, or shamanic state of consciousness—all essentially synonyms) is the mechanism through which many are invaded by demonic spirits.

Trance states are induced in various ways. Sometimes drugs and other substances are used to reach the trance state, as is common among shamans and Santeríans. Music is often the vehicle, with the beat of the drum and the dance that goes with it, as seen in "charismania" among Christians, where a person loses track of reality and "yields" to the spirit (assumed to be God's Holy Spirit). Books on Wicca and shamanism may come complete with chapters on various means to enter into the desired trance state so as to initiate the soul journey. They will invariably involve deep breathing, centering, visualizing, chanting, clearing of the mind, blanking out conscious thought from the mind, waiting to experience the otherworld, listening for the voice of a god, goddess, or spirit guide, dancing and whirling with eyes closed and heart ready to receive—whatever and whoever is out there. And the devil prowls around for just such a time and place to pounce.

My prior experience and recent research shows that the trance state is the most popular door opener to being possessed by demonic spirits.

HOW TO BECOME UNPOSSESSED OF DEMONS

Jesus alone has power over demons; all of the satanic kingdom is fully aware of this and trembles at His name. Excorcists are magicians who promise relief but succeed in little more than play acting, trickery, and deception.

Jesus' death on the cross, with His subsequent resurrection, ascension to heaven, and position at the right hand of the Father, has secured His power and authority over Satan and his fallen angels.

Consider two passages:

"The reason the Son of God appeared was to destroy the works of the devil" (1 John 3:8a).

"Since therefore the children share in flesh and blood, he himself likewise partook of the same things, that through death he might destroy the one who as the power of death, that is, the devil, and deliver all those who through fear of death were subject to lifelong slavery" (Hebrews 2:14-15).

Jesus cast demons out of people while on the planet two thousand years ago, and He gave His disciples authority to cast out demons as well:

"And he called the twelve together and gave them power and authority over all demons and to cure diseases, and he sent them out to proclaim the kingdom of God and to heal" (Luke 9:1-2).

Later Jesus sent out seventy-two others to do the same. (We see, then, that not only the Twelve called "apostles" had authority to cast out demons.) Upon their return the seventy-two gave the following report: "Lord, even the demons are subject to us in your name!" (Luke 10:17).

This authority over the demonic continues to this day. A key biblical verse in this regard is James 4:7: "Submit yourselves therefore to God. Resist the devil, and he will flee from you."

The verse's opening word, "Submit," is the largest stumbling block to many looking for a way out of the devil's sway. Demon possession gives power, and the demon will fight hard not to be cast out, so a usual ploy is to remind the person possessed that power will be lost. That threat freezes those who fear such a loss. The "submit" means a submission to the God and Father of our Lord Jesus Christ as well as a determined resistance to the devil. A spiritual battle ensues, until finally the demonic is rejected, Christ is embraced, and the demons flee.

If it is by the finger of God
That I cast out demons,
Then the kingdom of God
Has come upon you.

--Jesus, Luke 11:20

CHAPTER TEN

AFTER CARE

"When the unclean spirit has gone out of a person, it passes through waterless places seeking rest, and finding not he says, 'I will return to my house from which I came.' And when it comes, if finds the house swept and put in order. Then it goes and brings seven more evil that itself, and they enter and dwell there. And the last state of that person is worse than the first."

(This passage is from Luke 11:24-26, and there is a parallel passage at Matthew 12:43-45.)

It is highly probable that most of the people from whom Jesus cast out demons were not his followers; some may have been so but we have no direct information on the subject. However, with the demonic presence gone, what then? These same people would have been vulnerable to a re-possession, if we consider Jesus is correct about the restless unclean spirit—that is, unless they were born form above and indwelt by the Holy Spirit. This seems to be a legitimate commentary on the above passage.

The unclean spirit would be cast out but could return, and things would be worse than before.

Let us not assume that, if a person has demons cast out, then he or she will subsequently and automatically become a believer in and follower of Jesus. Maybe it is enough that the persistent turmoil subsides, even for a limited time period. I have witnessed this exact scenario a number of times. Perhaps the best one can do is present the message of the cross, pray that God will bring true conversion, and invite the person to remain in contact.

What more can be done?

DISCIPLESHIP

The normal Christian experience is to begin growing up into Christ-likeness upon conversion. This process is different for most of us, some growing more or less quickly than others. If a person does not have a home church, then efforts can be made to find one.

During the 1970s, the flood of those coming for deliverance from the demonic made it virtually impossible to properly pastor all those dear people. At times the best I could do was provide my telephone number, and sometimes not even that much.

It is not uncommon to find that those who have experienced the casting out of demons excel at ministering to others in the way they received mercy and grace. In fact, I have found that persons who have personally witnessed or experienced the power of Jesus to cast out Satan's minions make very strong Christians.

SMALL GROUP SUPPORT

Ideally, deliverance ministry will take place within a church congregation, where the normal ministries, services, worship, and fellowship are present.

Having demons cast out can be a shock to the system, characterized by disorientation and confusion. I am reminded of opening the proverbial Pandora's Box, out of which then emerged some very ugly things. Deliverance ministry actually needs to continue, perhaps for many years. There is a lot of unraveling to do; there may be deep wounds to be healed and memories from which to recover.

I have never been clear on the relationship between mental illness and demonic influence. That there can be both going on at once would hardly be surprising. If demons are cast out, other problems may surface. It should not be expected that following deliverance a person is now completely in his or her right mind. No, the deliverance ministry in its full extent may just be beginning.

It is best for small groups to be developed where people can talk about their experiences. This is what is called talk therapy, often run by the very people themselves without professionals. It is not a teaching or discipleship event; it is spiritual group therapy.

For thirty years I have operated a divorce recovery and loss workshop, all at Miller Avenue Church. What we do is simply provide a safe place to talk about what happened. Most often this is all that is necessary—to talk to others with a shared experience.

PROTECTING ANONYMITY AND CONFIDENTIALITY

Part of the strength of Twelve Step groups is their effort to ensure anonymity and confidentiality. Few will want the public, much less friends and family, to know what has happened to them. I have seen ministries "show-case" people, parading them about as though they were part of a circus, often to boost the ego of a minister.

There is a stigma attached to demonic possession, and it will never go away. There are those who do not mind who knows what, but for the majority—we need to guard each one's dignity.

GRACE AND MERCY

We are loved by God who has called us, justified us, and glorified us. Though we did not and do not deserve it, we are members of the household of God, and our names have been written—*permanently* written—in the Lamb's Book of Life.

And we never give up on each other. Parents do not throw their children out because they are loud, stinky, troublesome, rebellious, wrong, or crazy sometimes. God sticks with us through it all and sets us an example for the Church, bought with the blood of Jesus, to do the same.

EPILOGUE

No one really knows whether a Christian can have a demon. Indeed, no one really knows for sure if another person is, in fact, a Christian. Any pastor knows that there are members of the congregation who have been merely christianized and not genuinely converted. The visible Church is a mixed bag, and it is unsafe, from an eternal point of view, to base conclusions on slight evidence. Over the years my theological views have changed in regard to fringe points, and in matters where the Scripture is not entirely clear, a humble approach may be the best. Of paramount importance is the need of the suffering person to be freed from demonic influences.

It is never absolutely clear, whether someone asking for this ministry actually has demons; nevertheless, if a person asks for such a ministry there is no sufficient reason not to attempt it. It is quite simple really: if demons are there, then that will hopefully be found out, and they can be dealt with. If there are no demons present, then that is at least a comforting sign, and other issues can be explored.

The ministry of casting out of demons can be problematic. Some Christians have become somewhat arrogant or irreverent, thinking that they were quite something, that somehow the power over demons was theirs to wield and command. Others have become impatient with the struggles that those seeking release from demonic powers may exhibit. It is no small thing to put James 4:7 into practice, and this awareness and preparation is essential for deliverance ministry. Here is that verse again: "Submit yourself therefore to God. Resist the devil, and he will flee from you."

Most of the time spent in deliverance ministry is helping someone submit to God and resist Satan. It is not uncommon that a number of meetings are required over a span of weeks before a troubled person comes to the point where he or she begins to submit to God and resist the devil. The casting out of demons is a labor of love, definitely exhausting and time consuming; it is not for the faint of heart.

No one I have known who has experienced the power of Jesus casting demons out will question the reality of God and of the devil and his minions. That such a ministry even exists is a major problem for the devil, since his cover is completely blown and numbers of people will then have erased a large measure of doubt about eternal things.

That said, deliverance ministry is not a voyeuristic exercise. There are Christians, not having come to a secure and settled assurance of their salvation, who will want to be present when demons are cast out simply to provide a measure of assurance that Jesus is real. This ministry should have no viewer's gallery.

Some people—both Christians and non-Christians—will think anyone doing such work must be mad, whacko, crazy, and so on. There is no denying that from a worldly and secular point of view, such descriptive terms might be warranted. However, despite our possible amusement at gaining such a reputation, we are not playing to the audience in the stands but serving Him who is in heaven. It is a hearty person who dares commence the *work*—yes, hard *work*—of casting out of demons.

On the other hand, I have known well some who became proud of their so-called skill at casting demons out and who proclaimed their powerful anointing by God to do such ministry. Usually this ended badly, however, and I bring this up so others will not think more highly of themselves than they ought to.

One last thing: at Miller Avenue Baptist Church where I am pastor we have as part of our Sunday evening worship service a time for praying for those who are ill, based on James 5:13-15, and after the conclusion of the service, those who request the ministry of casting out of demons are invited to a separate and safe place for such work. At least two or more will remain later, sometimes much later, for such work. No one ever said Gospel ministry would always be neat and tidy, refreshing and dignified, applauded and published.

CPSIA information can be obtained at www.ICGtesting.com
Printed in the USA
BVOW04s1249151014

370845BV00002B/5/P

CPSIA information can be obtained
at www.ICGtesting.com
Printed in the USA
FFHW021329030619
52749421-58281FF